Phil Moser is a master at applying the Scriptures to everyday issues in such a way that people walk away with lives changed.

KEVIN O'BRIAN
Pastor, Ocean City Baptist Church

Phil Moser has done an admirable job of identifying spiritual principles and then applying them to daily life. I commend this work both to those struggling with their daily walk, and to those counselors who are seeking additional tools.

DR. JOHN MACARTHUR
Pastor-Teacher, Grace Community Church
President, The Master's Seminary

Hats off to Phil Moser for helping us navigate through life's most challenging issues in a clearly biblical way. The thing I like about these booklets is that they are forged by a pastor who has successfully wrestled through these issues with his flock, and thankfully he now shares them with the church at large.

DR. JOE STOWELL
President, Cornerstone University

It has been a high privilege to know Phil Moser for more than 20 years. He is one of today's most gifted communicators; possessing an unusual ability to deliver biblical truth in an intensely personal and practical way. Our guests and students rate him a perennial favorite. I can give no higher recommendation for your next conference or speaking opportunity.

DON LOUGH
Executive Director, Word of Life Fellowship

Pastor Phil's writing reflects a deep commitment to helping individuals both understand and obey God's Word in their daily life. As an experienced counselor he realizes that just teaching the truth is not enough; people need help on the practical steps of disciplining themselves for the purpose of godliness. I commend this combination of exposition, call to obedience and "how-to."

RANDY PATTEN
Director of Training and Advancement
Association of Certified Biblical Counselors

As an educator, Phil Moser is distinctively gifted. His pedagogical skill enables him to clearly explain very difficult concepts in understandable language that all learners can grasp. Audiences would greatly benefit by his teaching.

CAROL A. SHARP, PH.D.
Served as Dean of the College of Education 2002-2012
Rowan University, Glassboro, New Jersey

I have been greatly encouraged by Phil's teaching. When I listen to him, I always walk away with more. More knowledge, more insight, more understanding, more hope. He's my go-to-guy when I have questions about the Bible or Christian living.

MICHAEL BOGGS
Singer-Songwriter
Winner of Multiple Dove Awards

The Biblical Strategies materials have been a big plus for our adult classes. With the inclusion of the memory verse packs and accountability study guides, the materials lend themselves readily to the discipleship process.

STEVE WILLOUGHBY
Pastor, First Baptist Church of Patchogue, New York

Fighting the Fire

biblical strategies for overcoming anger

Phil Moser

Fighting the Fire: biblical strategies for overcoming anger

Published by Biblical Strategies.
Distributed by Send the Light.

Visit our Web site: www.biblicalstrategies.com.

© 2015 Phil Moser
International Standard Book Number: ISBN: 978-0-9905666-3-2

All rights reserved. No part of this book may be reproduced without prior written permission from the publisher, except where noted in the text and in the case of brief quotations embodied in critical articles and reviews.

Credits:
Cover Art: Gary Lizzi
Copy Editors: Wes Brown, Justin Carlton

Contributions:
The author wishes to express his gratitude to:
> The Association of Certified Biblical Counselors (ACBC) for their definitions of the various forms of anger that inspired "One Word isn't Enough" (pp. 9-28).
>
> A family of superheroes — Paul, Rayna, Mikaela and Mason Biester, Julie Moore, and Ashlyn Moser for their help in the images for "The Angry Man's Belief System" (pp. 30-34).
>
> Joe Schenke for his helpful insights for the 3 circles of responsibility (pp. 72-74).
>
> Jack Klose for his thought provoking questions that are a part of every accountability plan/study guide.

All Scripture quotations, unless otherwise indicated, are taken from THE HOLY BIBLE, English Standard Version. © 2001 Crossway Bibles, a ministry of Good News Publishers. Used by permission. All rights reserved.

Note: You may download a free accountability plan/study guide for *Fighting the Fire* by visiting biblicalstrategies.com. Choose the resource tab to print the guide and other tools.

Fighting the Fire

Striking the Match 7

Part 1: Think like God Thinks
   One Word isn't Enough
      Defining the key biblical terms 9
   Belief Really Does Matter
      Understanding the angry man's belief system. 29

Part 2: Do What Jesus Did
   Practicing Righteous Anger 35
   Avoiding Unrighteous Anger...................... 41

Part 3: Live by the Spirit
   How the Fruit of the Spirit Prevents Anger......... 47
   How the Armor of God Protects from Anger........ 51

Extinguishing the Fire 57

Practical Suggestions

Prayer
   Prayer patterns & names of God 59
Bible Study
   150 key replacement passages, 28-day reading schedule. 66
Scripture Retrieval
   20 key memory verses for overcoming anger 70
Holy Spirit Dependence
   3 circles of responsibility 72

Striking the Match

ALL IT TOOK was one match to light up the tinderbox that was the Colorado Rockies. Terry Barton claimed she struck that match to burn a letter she received from her estranged husband. The fire leaped outside of the fire ring, raced through the campsite, and eluded her attempt to put it out. The Hayman Fire, as it would come to be known, was the most costly fire in Colorado's history. It would surpass 39 million dollars, destroy 133 homes, and consume nearly 140,000 acres.[1] The consequences of Terry Barton striking one match were devastating. Barton was a forest ranger. She loved the wilderness. She knew the potential destruction that could come from her one simple act, but she believed that she would be the exception. Sadly, she was not.

If you struggle with anger, one simple act can wreak havoc on those you love the most. Once the fire starts burning, it feels beyond the scope of your will to stop it. It keeps burning—and a part of you wants it to. Later, when the fire subsides you look on the blackened ruin with regret. Your spouse is cold and averts your touch. Your daughter's eyes are furtive and fearful. Your friends make flimsy excuses for not wanting to be with you. There's even a memo in your file at work, a stark reminder that there can't be a next time. In spite of the grief you feel for your past actions, there's still a match in your hand, and you feel the familiar urge to strike it. When you look back at it, the wrong done to you doesn't seem to have justified your reaction, but it's so hard to remember that in the heat of the moment.

This is a book about how to live your life in such a way

that the landscape of your past will show more than charcoal and ashes. We will walk the pathway of change out of the blackened forest using three guidelines. We will learn to: (1) think like God thinks; (2) do what Jesus did; and (3) live by the Spirit. So why not join us? After all, you're not the only one standing there holding a match. So before you strike it again, why not learn how to put it down and leave the forest?

THINK LIKE GOD THINKS
One Word isn't Enough

THE BIBLE uses multiple words for anger. This is both helpful and convicting. Helpful, because it divides anger into parts that we can study, allowing us to discover the various ways it reveals itself. Convicting, because you may not have realized that you have an anger problem and you're about to find out that you do. Helpful, because once you have isolated the way your anger is expressed, you can start thinking about how to change. Convicting, because once you know how you should respond, you will be responsible to put it into practice. In Ephesians 4:31 we find six words that are associated with the angry person: Let all *bitterness* and *wrath* and *anger* and *clamor* and *slander* be put away from you, along with all *malice* [emphasis added]. In this chapter we will discover the meaning of each of these words, and learn how to indentify a more godly quality to replace it.

(1) Bitterness: a stubborn refusal to release those who have hurt you.

The word "bitter" was used in the Bible to describe the bitter herb that the Jews would take at Passover as a reminder of their cruel and bitter treatment in Egypt when they served Pharaoh as slaves.[2] The prophet Jeremiah used the word to describe his refusal to celebrate or rejoice with those around him. He was insistent on being alone.[3] In Biblical times the Greeks used a word to describe bitterness that meant, "a long-standing resentment, as the spirit which refuses to be reconciled."[4] Nelson Mandela once said, "Resentment is like drinking poison and then hoping it will kill your enemies."[5]

A bitter person is consciously, willfully angry. He refuses to let a hurt go. He insists on making the other person pay. Whereas, the Bible instructs us to set our mind on the Spirit of God,[6] the bitter person refuses to let go of his pain. As he dwells upon how he was wronged, he convinces himself that his anger is justified. Being fully convinced of his interpretation of the facts in his own mind, he secretly continues to accuse his offender. As he does this, the bitterness grows. Soon it effects other areas of his life as well.

Sometimes that bitterness isn't focused on a human offender, but on one's circumstances. This was the case for Naomi (her story is told in the book of Ruth). Death had first taken her husband, then her two sons.[7] She even changed her name from Naomi to Mara (meaning bitterness) to reflect her anger. Naomi exemplifies the kind of person who has grown bitter over life's circumstances. But, because God in his sovereignty is in control of all circumstances,[8] this kind of person is ultimately directing her disapproval towards God. While a forgiving spirit is the replacement for a bitter one, it is important to remember the Bible never speaks of us *forgiving* God. Forgiveness is offered to those who have intentionally wronged us.[9] God has not done so, nor could he.[10] The biblical character, Job and the Old Testament prophet Habakkuk were individuals who perceived God to have acted unjustly and addressed him as such. But God revealed his true character to them, and both men repented. Throughout the Psalms we meet those who are genuinely struggling under difficult circumstances—and they share this openly,[11]—but with few exceptions they conclude their grievances by remembering and affirming some aspect about the character of God.[12] That is the proper way to deal with one's bitterness towards God.

Bitterness's replacement: Forgiveness

On the human front, the biblical strategy for overcoming bitterness is forgiveness. Forgiveness is making a commitment to release the offender from the punishment you believe they deserve for the hurt they've caused.[13] Often the bitter person will insist that the offender doesn't deserve forgiveness. This places the angry person in the judge's seat and only further fuels his bitterness. The Bible, however, doesn't teach that you forgive your offender because they deserve it. Instead, it teaches that you forgive someone because you were yourself forgiven by God when you deserved it least. In the verse immediately following our passage of study we read, "Be kind to one another, tenderhearted, *forgiving one another, even as God in Christ has forgiven you* [emphasis added].[14]

Once when I was teaching on forgiveness, a woman sought my counsel afterwards. She had a cynical response to my teaching. She insisted that there were some hurts that were so deep that they couldn't be forgiven. Later that week we met, and she shared her sad story. Her brother was serving a prison sentence for a crime he'd committed against their family. In her bitterness, she had never visited him during his incarceration, and now he was about to be released. As I listened to her resentment, it struck me that her brother wasn't the only one imprisoned. I told her so, and she wept. After some time, she lifted her head, looked me in the eyes and said, "How do I get out?" I took a deep breath, knowing we were in painful territory. "Have you ever confronted him for his wrongdoing, shared your pain, and told him he should ask your forgiveness?" She shook her head. "Do you know why you haven't done that?" She shook her head again. "Perhaps you're afraid that he might actually ask; then you'd have a choice to make." The statement hung in the air until her voice interrupted the silence: "Well, I think we're done here." I walked her to the door, and thanked her for the courage to share such a painful experience. Two weeks later following a service, I saw her across the sanctuary. She was walking briskly towards me, her dour frown replaced with a broad smile. "I did it," she said. "I visited my brother in prison, and I released him from the hurt he had caused." "He's free," then thoughtfully she added, "And so am I."

Five years later I was speaking at another church when I looked into the audience and saw the same woman. She still wore the same smile she had for our last meeting. After the service she thanked me again for encouraging her to restore the relationship with her brother. "He died two years after he was released from prison," she said. "I'm so thankful I was able to restore my relationship with him after all those years." As she introduced me to her other brother who was with her, he said, "Thank you for setting my sister free. For years she was trapped in her pain." As they turned to walk away, it occurred to me: *bitterness is a prison cell of our own making, and forgiveness is the only key that opens the prison door.*

(2) Wrath: Flaring Outbursts of Anger

The biblical term for "wrath" is understood as flaring outbursts of anger. It comes from the Greek word *thymos*, denoting a violent movement of air, water, or earth.[15] As such, it is a good picture of the type of anger that is often hidden or unexpected until it becomes explosive. Earthquakes catch us unaware; tornadoes don't forecast their destinations; tsunamis can't be predicted. These natural disasters also suggest the violence and destruction implied by the word. When an earthquake hits, centuries of development can be reduced to rubble in a few seconds. *Thymos* is descriptive of the type of destruction that accompanies the person with an unrestrained temper.

Throughout the Bible this word is translated as "wrath," "fury," "anger," "passion," or "enraged."[16] Many of its instances in the New Testament describe God's righteous response to continual, unrepentant sin.[17] Ten of the 18 times it occurs are in the book of Revelation, where John recounts his vision of God justly settling all accounts at the end of the age. Because the Bible declares God as perfect,[18] his judgment and his accompanying actions would be as well. Therefore, God is justified in bringing his righteous wrath to bear on those who had rebelled against him. Wrath describes the destructive end result of judgment. Because our judgment—unlike God's—is imperfect, the Bible discourages our expressions of wrath.[19] Here are a few of the key Scriptures:

- Let all bitterness and *wrath* and anger and clamor and slander be put away from you, along with all malice.[20]
- But now you must put them all away: anger, *wrath*, malice, slander, and obscene talk from your mouth.[21]
- Now the works of the flesh are evident, which are: adultery, fornication, uncleanness, lewdness, idolatry, sorcery, hatred, contentions, jealousies, outbursts of *wrath* [emphasis added].[22]

The father who explodes with angry words at his 9-year-old's soccer game has made some type of *judgment*. Perhaps he has judged the referee for a missed call; the coach for not giving his son more playing time; or his son for not putting forth his best effort. We refer to this process as *losing your temper*, but in truth, a judgment took place first. That judgment was followed by a response. If we only address the flare of temper, success will be short lived. We are mistaken if we assume it was caused by the circumstance. It is important to remember the angry outburst was preceded by our *judgment* of the circumstance. We faced a conflict, and something in us said, "That isn't right!" Because it didn't appear as if anyone else noticed this injustice, our temper flared, broadcasting our disapproval to whomever was within shouting distance. I call this a *thymos* moment, and it happens so fast that it feels like a singular event. But in truth, it is a judgment followed by a response. Think of it like an earthquake: the tectonic plates shift miles below the earth's surface, and moments later your house shakes violently. In much the same way, our judgment is followed by a response. Our overconfidence in a quick and often irrational judgment makes the temper seem justified.

Wrath's replacement: Patience

But the Bible reminds us that we shouldn't always be so confident in our subjective assessment of a situation. Perhaps our judgment is wrong. We need to patiently wait for God to act. Notice the caution of the Scriptures in regards to one's overconfidence:

Bless those who persecute you; bless and do not curse [...] Do not set your mind on high things, but associate with the humble. *Do not be wise in your own opinion.* Repay no one evil for evil [...] If it is possible, as much as depends on you, live peaceably with all men [...] Do not avenge yourselves, but rather give place to wrath [God's wrath]; for it is written, "Vengeance is Mine, I will repay," says the Lord [emphasis added].[23]

To overcome your desire to reveal your anger, you must leave room for God to act. He alone is positioned to make the most thorough and accurate judgment, and respond appropriately. In *The Message*, Eugene Peterson translates Romans 12:19: "Don't insist on getting even; that's not for you to do. 'I'll do the judging,' says God. 'I'll take care of it.'"

In order to overcome a quick, violent temper, you must be patient in the moment you form a judgment, not just when your temper flares. It's not easy, but God has given us the Holy Spirit to guide us through precisely these kinds of challenging situations. Live in the humble reality that you may not have all the details. Admit you don't know everything the other person is thinking. Don't just automatically assume your judgment is accurate. Ask questions before you make accusations. Remember the words of Scripture: *Do not be wise in your own opinion.* Though you are not all-wise, God is. So replace your quick temper with thoughtful patience. Before you shout out your opinion, give God time to share his.

(3) Anger: a settled indignation—a slow burn

While *thymos* describes the kind of anger that explodes and leaves destruction in it's wake, there is another type of anger that is even more dangerous. The Greek word *orge* describes the anger of a person who is taking a long time to think about how he will respond. While he's taking time, he isn't seeking a spiritual replacement or patiently waiting for God.[24] Instead, he is hunkering down in his hurt, judgment, and indignation. Bible commentator William Barclay refers to *orge* as,

> A long-lived anger ... the anger of the man who nurses his wrath to keep it warm; it is the anger over which a person broods, and which he will not allow to die.[25]

This is the anger of the person who has become fully convinced he has a right to be angry.

When we dwell upon how we believe we were wronged, we develop a sense of entitlement. This is the kind of entitlement the prophet Jonah had as he sat on a hillside outside of Nineveh and longed for that city's destruction.[26] In the end, God asked Jonah the question, "Do you do well to be angry?"[27] He responded with, "Yes, I do well to be angry, angry enough to die."[28] This is *orge* anger. There is conviction in it. This person will not be easily persuaded that they are wrong. They are too deeply invested in the conclusion to surrender it easily. Like Jonah, when we choose to dwell upon how we were wronged we will find anger to be a trap—a warm and inviting one, perhaps, but a trap nonetheless. That is why Paul warns fellow believers to "put them all away: anger, wrath, malice, slander..."[29] James offers the same insistence when he says,

> Know this, my beloved brothers: let every person be quick to hear, slow to speak, slow to anger; for the anger of man does not produce the righteousness of God."[30]

Most people think of anger as only an emotion, so they strive to control it only at the emotional level. Interestingly, the popular culture describes love in much the same way, as more emotion than volition.[31] But while anger and love do touch our emotional side, they are not exclusively feelings. The Bible defines responses like anger and love more as choices than emotions. William Barclay's definition of the word *orge* makes this clear. The angry person is brooding, meditating and dwelling upon the things that make him angry. He is choosing to think thoughts that stir up angry responses. Imagine it this way: your thoughts are the fuel for your emotions, and your emotions become the basis for your conviction. As you brood and dwell upon your hurt, you are fueling those emotions. As you fuel the emotions, they seem to burn hotter. It feels like they are happening to you, as if you are a passive recipient in the process, not an active one. It's easy to forget—albeit temporarily—that you are the one stoking the fire of your emotions with your thoughts.

The growing fire of our emotions bring about another result. Because our emotions *feel* so genuine, we are more likely to believe that they are based on truth. In reality, they are only based upon our thoughts. In our arrogance, we presume that our thoughts are based upon truth. This is why Jonah expressed such conviction that he had a right to be angry, even when he didn't. He had dwelt upon what he perceived to be wrong for so long that he was convinced it was true. Ironically, he had experienced firsthand the mercy of God, and he affirmed that truth about God's character.[32] Yet, in his anger, he stubbornly refused to allow the truth about God's mercy to be granted to the Ninevites. Jonah, the preacher of the greatest revival in the history of mankind, rejected the chance to rejoice in the sparing of a people and insisted upon their destruction. Jonah was unwilling to let his thoughts be brought into line with those of a gracious, merciful God. Had he done so, he would have stopped fueling the fire of his emotions and weakened his mistaken conviction. Sadly, he did not. As long as we are of sound mind, our thought processes are always choices, even if they don't feel that way.[33] In order to gain consistent victory over *orge* anger, you will need to do more than work on your emotions: you will need to rebuild your belief system (see "Belief Really Does Matter", p. 29-34).

Anger's replacement: Love

Because this type of anger is a choice, we can choose to replace it with thoughts and actions that make way for real transformation. Though our culture perceives anger and love to be more about what we feel than what we choose, the Bible tells us that both are primarily choices—love naturally replaces anger. When we believe we've been wronged, it's easy to feel unloved. Our thoughts swirl around our hurt and pain. But what if there was message that was so bold, so strong, so efficacious that it overwhelmed your sense of entitlement? A message that reminded you, without a doubt, you were loved. Such is the gospel message: *For God so loved the world, that he gave his only Son, that whoever believes in him should not perish but have eternal life.*[34] Dwelling upon God's love is a powerful replacement to dwelling upon your angry, indignant thoughts. The life Jesus lived testifies of this. He was:

- Abandoned by his closest friends in his hour of need.[35]
- Betrayed by a close confidant after years of his investment[36]
- Rejected by the religious leaders for their political gain.[37]
- Turned upon by the fickle crowd that five days earlier had heralded his arrival as king[38]

Any one of these challenges would have stirred up in us an unrighteous anger. Yet, notice where Jesus had directed his thoughts. In his final recorded prayer in John 17 we read, "because you have loved me before the foundation of the world."[39] By dwelling on the Father's love, Jesus was able to respond graciously to the most violent of rejections. The one who had created[40] and sustained[41] all things did not take upon himself the mantle of entitlement, but rather the form of a servant.

> Have this mind among yourselves, which is yours in Christ Jesus, who, though he was in the form of God, did not count equality with God a thing to be grasped, but emptied himself, by taking the form of a servant, being born in the likeness of men. And being found in human form, he humbled himself by becoming obedient to the point of death, even death on a cross.[42]

As he meditated on the Father's love, he was able to love others well, and avoid the temptation to be sinfully angry.[43] Can you imagine the possibilities if we would consistently follow Christ's example?

(4) Clamor: contentious, public quarreling.

Bitterness, wrath and anger start as internal expressions of anger, but they don't remain that way. They soon manifest themselves in our relationships. When those relationships become contentious and we quarrel publicly, then *clamor* is the word that describes them. It is what anger looks like when it erupts verbally between friends or family. Peace is gone, replaced with over-talking, interrupting, and arguing. Our English word *clamor* translates the Greek word *krauge*. The root word means "to cry out loud."[44] The Greek word is actually onomatopoeic—meaning it sounds like what it is. It is meant to sound like a raven's cry.[45]

I grew up in rural Indiana, where, as a middle school student, I would drop off my books at our house and head into the woods the moment school was out. Those long walks in the woods were peaceful and quiet. While our woods were filled with wildlife, the animals would go into stealth mode when they sensed a human presence. The only sound I would hear was the crunching of autumn leaves beneath my Converse high-tops. Then, out of nowhere, a crow's cry would pierce the silence, alerting all in the forest that he had seen an intruder. Even when I anticipated that old crow's cry, I would nearly jump out of my sneakers. His voice interrupted the wood's tranquility. This is the idea behind this word clamor. Our angry, public quarreling breaks the peaceful silence.

Throughout the Old and New Testaments, the word *clamor* is filled with emotion; from the unrestrained crying of the Egyptians at the loss of their firstborn sons,[46] to the public outcry of the angry crowds in Ephesus.[47] But while it may aptly describe a publicly expressed angst, it can also describe a wrong way of speaking in personal relationships. The context of Ephesians 4:31 suggests that "clamor" just as easily describes conversations had in your home, the workplace, or even church. Perhaps you've taken part in conversations where there were incessant interruptions, each over-talking the other. Where declaring your opinion matters more than your partner finishing their sentence. When interrupting doesn't work, we simply raise the volume on what we say. When the other party refuses to hear us, we just regurgitate the same idea, as if interruption, shouting, and repetition somehow make our argument more convincing. To those observing, we sound like the crow flying off through a peaceful wood. Our incessant *caw-cawing* serves no purpose but to raise the level of the clamor.

Clamor's replacement: thoughtful listening

The Bible's answer to decreasing the level of clamor in your relationships is to increase the level of thoughtful listening. James captured it this way: Let every person be quick to hear, slow to speak, slow to anger; for the anger of man does not produce the righteousness of God.[48]

Honoring Others

When we disagree with someone, it's often tempting to interrupt them. But if I'm unwilling to let you finish your sentence, it's usually because I'm thinking too highly of my own opinion.[49] I believe that what I have to say should trump what you have to say. Hear James' warning again: we ought to be *quick* to hear and s*low* to speak [emphasis added]. His statement implies that we should not simply listen perfunctorily or wait for an opportunity to control the conversation. Rather, we should genuinely seek to understand what the other person is saying. In his book *The Seven Habits of Highly Effective People*, Steven Covey captured this idea in eight memorable words: *seek first to understand, then to be understood*.[50] The sincere practice of those words will bring an end to clamor. This is what thoughtful listening looks like. Understanding what another has to say should be more important than getting them to understand what we have to say. That does not mean that we'll always come to agreement. It does mean, however, that we will have listened first and spoken last. While we may not have fully understood the other person's position, at least we have sought to do so. Clamoring loses its fervor when even one member of the conversation adopts this posture.

Growing in wisdom

Clamoring is about making our opinion known at the expense of another. As our clamoring grows in intensity, it often reveals odd bedfellows: ignorance and arrogance. Perhaps you've seen the bumper sticker: *Better to remain silent and be thought a fool, then to speak out and remove all doubt.* The one who thinks to highly of his own opinion[51] will not see his need to grow in wisdom. His mind is made up. Such arrogance is not only a stumbling block to good listening, but to learning as well. If we do not see the value in listening to others, we will sacrifice the opportunity to gain wisdom from others. Several of the Proverbs make that abundantly clear:

- When words are many, transgression is not lacking, but whoever restrains his lips is prudent.[52]
- Whoever restrains his words has knowledge, and he who has a cool spirit is a man of understanding.[53]
- If one gives an answer before he hears, it is his folly and shame.[54]

To avoid clamor, work at becoming a more thoughtful listener. In so doing, you will reflect honor on the one who is speaking, and gain wisdom from what is said.

(5) Slander: speech intended to injure.

In my work as a pastor, I've met some very angry people. Initially, I may not know why they're so angry, but if I can get them talking—and I listen carefully—I can often discover why they think they are. One of the keys for me is to probe those moments when they are willing to slander somebody. A wife will say, "You *never* do that," and her husband will respond, "You're such a *liar*." Both are guilty of slander—they are choosing their words intentionally to hurt the other person.

Slander is defined as "making a false spoken statement that is damaging to another's reputation."[55] When they're angry, most people do this quite naturally without giving it a second thought. Nevertheless, a technical understanding of some of the ways we move from truth to falsehood (the first step of slander) is beneficial if you want to change. Here's my top-three list from years of helping people change.

Number 1: Take the statement out of context, and give it your own meaning.

Truth always has a context. One of the simplest ways to turn truth to falsehood is to remove a statement from its context and give it a different intention. You can probably remember a time in your life when you were being quoted and you responded, "That is what I said, but it's not what I meant." Someone had simply taken your statement out of context and given it a meaning of their own.

I once heard the story of a big-city mobster whose brother, Harry—with whom he had been a partner in crime—had died. When the mobster met with the minister that would be doing the funeral, he insisted that Harry be eulogized as "a saint." The minister was troubled with this statement, because he didn't know how he could include it and maintain his integrity. While preparing the eulogy, an idea came to him. He smiled and jotted it down. The day of the funeral arrived, and the minister stepped to the pulpit, the mobster brother sitting in the front pew. His eulogy was kind, but truthful. He did not deny the crimes the brother had committed nor whitewash his actions. The mobster brother grew increasingly uncomfortable—Harry was not being made out to be a saint. The minister came to the end of his sermon, closed his notes, and said, "I have attempted to be truthful in recounting Harry's life. As you know, it was filled with heinous crimes and vile actions, but compared to his brother here" he gestured to the front row, "*Harry was a saint.*"

While the story is humorous, the implication of this tactic in relationships is not. Words, taken out of the their context and given another meaning become falsehoods. When people slander each other, marriages become toxic, children can become divisive, and families can crumble. Take a statement out of context, lace it with evil intent, add your own meaning, then tell it over and over again. Soon, those around you will began to believe what you believe. Simply put, it's just not that hard to slander another person.

Number 2: Change verbs into nouns.

It's probably safe to say, "At some point in our lives, we have all been dishonest"—either in what we said or in what we didn't say.[56] But the fact that you've been dishonest in the past doesn't necessarily make you a liar categorically. When we describe a person's behavior in the moment, we use verbs; when a person's behavior is characterized by a certain action, we switch to nouns. For example, I've played golf a couple of dozen times in my life, but I can assure you that doesn't make me a golfer. Just ask those who've played with me. Saying, "I've golfed" is very different than saying "I'm a golfer." It would be arrogant for me to claim the title because I am not characterized as a golfer. Conversely, it is arrogant for us to call someone by a name when they are not characterized by the action. This is slander—and it harms the reputation of the person we are speaking to or about. From a Christian's perspective, even if the person repeats the offense, but acknowledges wrong doing and repents,[57] we should extend grace and forgive.[58]

Number 3: Use 100% language

Words like *always* and *never* are 100% language, and when they are used critically in a relationship they are rarely (see I didn't say never) true. These words often show up when two people are distressed by each other's behavior. Each may feel that their ideas are not being taken seriously, that something important to them isn't being recognized, or that they simply aren't being treated as they should. In that kind of relationship, the words occur so frequently, that I have learned to listen for them as a counselor. A wife will say, "He *never* picks up his clothes." Her husband will counter, "She is *always* spending money." Usually when these words are used, I can envision the partner's mental hard drive spinning. They are looking for the one occurrence when they did pick up their cloths or check the budget before they went shopping. They respond, "That's not true! Don't you remember when..."

Words like "always" and "never" are used to characterize the person. When you speak like this, you are slandering. You are making a false spoken statement that is damaging to another's reputation.

Slander's replacement: grace and truth

Taking words out of their context, changing verbs into

nouns, and using 100% language are all verbal expressions of an angry heart. This happens naturally when we're angry. To overcome slander, we will need a supernatural replacement. We find one in Jesus. He was characterized as being full of grace and truth.[59] When we slander, we are being neither gracious nor truthful. We are untruthful because we exaggerate or rip somebody's words from their context. We are ungracious because our intention is to tear down, not build up.[60] Gracious words give the benefit of the doubt; they hope all things,[61] and they edify. Notice Paul's words to the Ephesians,

> Let no corrupting talk come out of your mouths, but only such as is good for building up, as fits the occasion, that it may give grace to those who hear.[62]

(6) Malice is the desire to harm others.

Malice is a harsh word. It even sounds mean. The U.S. legal system gives it clear definition:

> Malice in law is the intent, without justification excuse or reason, to commit a wrongful act that will result in harm to another. Malice means the wrongful intention and includes all types of intent that law deems to be wrongful. Legally speaking any act done with a wrong intention is done maliciously.[63]

Notice the definition's focus on *intent*. Often the court will determine the degree of the crime by whether or not intent can be determined.[64] The Bible also understands malice to include the idea of intent. It uses words like "evil" and "wickedness" to define the intent of malice.[65] Malice doesn't develop overnight. There is a process that starts when we don't get what we desire. I have often referred to this as the "selfish staircase." We start with unmet desires, and those desires fuel the changes that keep leading us further

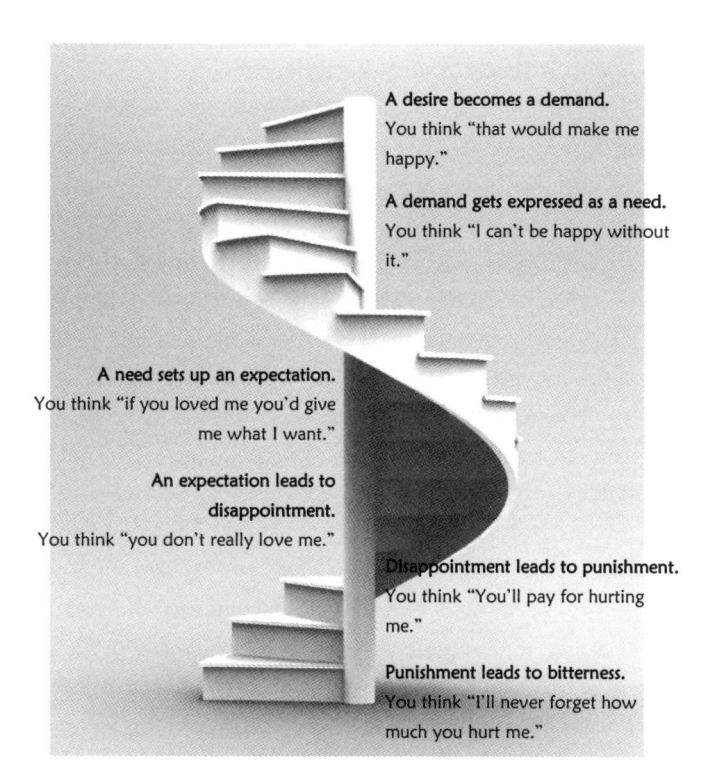

A desire becomes a demand.
You think "that would make me happy."

A demand gets expressed as a need.
You think "I can't be happy without it."

A need sets up an expectation.
You think "if you loved me you'd give me what I want."

An expectation leads to disappointment.
You think "you don't really love me."

Disappointment leads to punishment.
You think "You'll pay for hurting me."

Punishment leads to bitterness.
You think "I'll never forget how much you hurt me."

down. Eventually we come to the basement where malice and bitterness reside. Notice that each of the steps downward is marked with what we perceive or think. This is important: anger starts with an expectation that, when unrealized, leads to disappointment. The severity of that disappointment awakens within me the desire to punish whoever hurt me. But that punishment only leads to bitterness, because, when my emotions are fueled by hurt, I lack the objectivity necessary for reasonable justice. Punishment, especially the kind that is driven by malice, can never heal the wound that was caused by another — it can only wound the other.

Malice's replacement: kind deeds

The Bible does offer a solution to overcome malice, and it is not justice. Read carefully Paul's words to the Romans,

> Beloved, never avenge yourselves, but leave it to the wrath of God, for it is written, "Vengeance is mine, I will repay, says the Lord." To the contrary, "if your enemy is hungry, feed him; if he is thirsty, give him something to drink; for by so doing you will heap burning coals on his head." Do not be overcome by evil, but overcome evil with good.[66]

The replacement for malice is acts of kindness. In acting kindly, we leave room for God's justice,[67] secure in the promise that our heart will not grow hard, but more sensitive to the needs of others.

In the movie *Fireproof*, Kirk Cameron plays a husband who is emotionally detached from his wife. She, in turn, looks to another man for her emotional fulfillment. While Cameron's character could have returned evil for evil, he instead takes the "40-day love dare" —a commitment to do a simple act of kindness every day for his wife for 40 days in a row. Those simple acts of kindness protect his heart from hardening, open him up to genuinely love his wife, and eventually causes her to renew her commitment to their marriage.

Having seen similar responses from real life couples, I can assure you this is more than a Hollywood story. Acts of kindness weaken malice and overcome evil with good.

Belief Really Does Matter
Understanding the angry man's belief system

B ECAUSE anger is a mixture of our emotions, thoughts and choices, it often feels like something that happens to us. Our prideful tendency is to shift the blame to others, causing us to feel justified in our victimhood. We express this position when we say things like, "You make me so mad," or "I wouldn't get angry if you didn't treat me like that." But are we willing to relinquish that level of control to another person? Is that what we really believe?[68] In the moment it might *feel* that way, but is it an accurate expression of what is really happening? Recall from our study of the word "clamor" that when we practice an unrestrained expression of our feelings, we become more confident that their motivations are truthful, and we quit trying to discern whether or not they actually are.

The Greek language is, among other things, very descriptive. Its verbs communicate meaning through mood, form, voice, and tense. The voice of the verb indicates the doer and/or receiver of the action. In the case of anger the active voice would read, "I made you angry;" whereas, the passive voice would read "I was made angry by you." In the first case, I was the doer of the action; in the second case, I was the receiver of the action. But the Greek language, unlike English, also has a middle voice where one can be both the doer *and* the receiver of an action. The Bible scholar W.E. Vine makes a significant point about the word "anger." He notes that eight of the times it occurs in the Scripture, it is in the middle voice.[69] In those instances, it literally means, "I made myself angry by what you did."

What makes this Biblical truth so challenging to grasp is that anger rarely *feels* that way. It genuinely feels like: *I was made angry by you.*

Let me illustrate with an imaginary character by the name of Jack. Jack has anger problems. He knows it. His boss knows it, and most significantly, his family knows it. Like all of us, Jack's inner life is comprised of his thoughts, emotions, and choices. But because of the deceptive nature

of emotion, it always feels like circumstances are conspiring against him. And because he determines truth largely by how he feels, he believes other people are causing his anger. It's almost as if he's not an active participant. The reason Jack feels this way is that when he's angry, his thoughts seem to run on their own; he doesn't feel in control of his emotions. The only thing left of Jack's inner identity is his choices. Yet, with his thoughts and emotions fueled by his anger, it feels as if his choices have been taken away as well. He's even expressed it this way: *I don't have a choice but to get angry.* Jack feels like he's boxed in. We might even think of him as "Jack-in-the-box."

But the Bible teaches that Jack isn't trapped in a box where his emotions, thoughts, and choices are decided for him. Notice the propositional statements of Scripture:

- It is for freedom that Christ has set us free.[70]
- I can do all things through Christ who strengthens me.[71]
- Or do you not know that you are the slave of whatever you choose to obey?[72]
- For you were called to freedom, brothers...through love serve one another.[73]

As a believer, a better presentation of Jack would look like the image below.

Jack is set free to engage his emotions, thoughts and choices as he will. He received a new heart at the point of salvation.[74] That new heart, filled with the Spirit of God, enables him to set his thoughts upon Christ,[75] engage his emotions around the things of God,[76] and make choices in light of the will of God.[77] Certainly this is a process, and I would not want to infer that an emotional change takes place overnight. Still, our emotions usually follow what we have chosen to think about. With his new heart, Jack can now make choices and think differently than he did before. This is a theological reality that is incredibly freeing. But, when Jack is angry, it doesn't feel that way. From his perspective in the box, it feels like anger is happening to him—like others are causing his anger. His son's refusal to do his homework consumes his thoughts, his daughter's belligerence fuels his emotions; and when his wife greets him at the door with a honey-do list, Jack feels like his choices for the weekend have already been made for him. As shown below, from where Jack stands in the box, it feels like his thoughts, emotions, and choices are out of his control.

When anger is at work, he doesn't *feel* free in Christ. He believes he has no other choice but to get angry. Because of our tendency to shift the blame for our wrongdoing to others, we are prone to interpret our anger in the passive voice. We are quick to say, "You *make me* so angry when you do that." This is the angry man's belief system: he believes that others are causing his anger. But remember that the Bible speaks of anger occurring in the middle voice. So, to bring what you believe in line with what the Bible is teaching, you need to say, "I make myself so angry when you do that." While Jack's anger feels like the image

on the opposite page what is actually happening is shown above. Jack believes he is in a box because of what others are doing, but the truth is that he is the one controlling his thoughts, emotions, and choices. Biblically speaking, Jack's anger occurs in the middle voice—he is the one causing it. This is why you will never overcome anger without first correcting your belief system. While anger feels like something that's happening to you, it is actually something that you are doing to yourself. Your belief system matters. When you think about how you were wronged, you feel more justified in your belief system, and anger naturally follows. If you meditate on anything long enough, you will begin to believe it. The order matters: thinking leads to belief, belief fuels your emotions, and the emotions erupt in angry speech, actions, and attitude.

Understanding anger in the middle voice actually brings great hope. You are free in Christ, even when it doesn't feel that way. Work on bringing your belief system in line with the Scriptures; bring every thought captive, and you will discover that he who the Son sets free is free indeed.

DO WHAT JESUS DID
Practicing Righteous Anger

THE FERVOR in Jerusalem was palpable. Jesus was in town, and everyone knew it. He had arrived on Sunday to cheering crowds.[78] Once in the city, he ascended to the Temple Mount, looked around, then left Jerusalem and returned to Bethany.[79] It was the next day that the trouble would begin.

Because it was the week of Passover, the city was packed with travelers. Inns got double the going rate, and everything needed to celebrate Passover was in short supply. The law of supply and demand drove prices up all over town. It was no wonder that the high priest wanted in on the action. After all, he controlled the best real estate in the whole city—the temple courtyard, known as the court of the Gentiles. He rented the merchants their table locations and took a cut of all they sold. Why shouldn't he profit? This was the time of year that everybody else would.

Jesus returned from his restful night at Bethany with one goal in mind.[80] As he ascended the step of the temple, he could hear the bartering of the merchants mingled with the complaints of his people. "These prices are an outrage," one man shouted. "They take my hard earned money to line the silk pockets of the high priest!" added another. Jesus walked past them, his eyes focused intently on the nearest table. "Back of the line, Mister!" the merchant barked. Jesus' hand reached for the edge of the table. He tested its weight, remembering the tables in his father's woodshop. The merchant, intent on counting his money, didn't even look up. "I said get to the back of the ..." his voice hung in the air for the table was gone. He stared in disbelief. The heavy table lay upside down in the middle of the courtyard. His carefully placed stacks of coins were still scattering across the veranda when he heard the second table go, followed by another. Jesus' voice was anything but gentle as it rose above the commotion. "It's meant to be a house of prayer, but you have made it a hangout for thieves! Get out of my Father's house! And stop cheating my people!"[81]

The Bible records several occasions when Jesus was angry,[82] yet it also maintains that he never sinned.[83] We are right to surmise, then, that there must be a time for righteous anger. While Jesus was not characterized by anger, the few times that he grew angry are instructive—they show us what righteous anger looks like.

Jesus' primary concern was others, particularly the weak and underprivileged.

There were two ways in which the religious leaders were abusing others that deeply troubled Jesus. First, they were taking advantage of the location of the Temple at Passover to sell animal sacrifices and exchange money at an exorbitant rate. Second, they had overtaken the court of the Gentiles—a location intended for prayer for the pagan nations—and made it a market. If you you've ever been to an airport, then you understand that something remarkable happens once you pass through security. The prices on all products and services increase dramatically. Sometimes it takes less than 100 feet for those prices to go up. The convenience for not having to go back through security has a price tag, and its attached to everything from your chicken sandwich to your toothpaste. Likewise, in Jesus' time, a similar kind of extortion was taking place, but it came at the hands of the key religious leaders: Annas and Caiaphas. Here is how they used their power to take advantage of the poor and enrich their coffers:

> Annas was a member of the Sadducees, the aristocracy of first century Judea. He shared their characteristics of being arrogant, ambitious, and having enormous wealth, which they used to maintain their political control. His family was notorious for their greed [...] The family of Annas had gained much of their wealth from the four "booths of the sons of Annas", which were market stalls located on the Mount of Olives. They also had other market stalls inside the temple complex, in the Court of the Gentiles. Through these, they had a monopoly on the sale of sacrificial animals, as well as on the exchanging of money into temple coins for the offerings. This enabled them to charge exorbitant prices, effectively gaining their wealth through the exploitation and oppression of the poor.[84]

Jesus came to offer hope to the weak and underprivileged. He spent his life serving them, not taking advantage of them.[85] This was characteristic of God the Father. The Psalmist described him as the "Father of the fatherless and protector of widows." God is the one who "leads out the prisoners to prosperity."[86] It should come as no surprise to us that Jesus, too, would have a special place in his heart for the weak and underprivileged. He came to serve them, not be served by them.[87] This was not the case with the religious leaders of Jesus' day. They had no qualms with taking advantage of the weak and underprivileged and profiting from their difficult circumstances. The poor grew poorer, and the religious leaders grew wealthier.

This angered Jesus, and rightly so. Both Matthew and Mark specifically note that Jesus overturned the tables of those who were selling doves.[88] Doves were the sacrifice that the poorest of the Israelites would bring to the temple. From Jesus' perspective, to take advantage of the poorest of the poor was unconscionable. The religious leaders' wealth mongering knew no limits. Jesus modeled a righteous anger that was quick to protect others.

A friend of mine once observed, "Righteous anger has a very short shelf life. It's like leaving milk out of the refrigerator overnight. You probably won't want to put in on your breakfast cereal in the morning."[89] Jesus' righteous anger was similarly short-lived. The gospel writers recount that, after entering Jerusalem on Palm Sunday, Jesus walked around the temple and then returned to Bethany for the night.[90] The next morning he returned to Jerusalem, ascended the temple mount, and began overturning tables.[91] Righteous anger is meant to elicit an immediate response on behalf of the weak and weary. Just as milk turns sour if it's not used immediately, so righteous anger turns unrighteous (bitterness, wrath, anger, clamor, slander, malice) if we don't respond promptly.[92]

Biblical counselor David Powlison provides a useful diagnostic tool in his pamphlet[93] on anger. He asks seven questions that can help us determine whether our anger is righteous or unrighteous:

- Do you get angry about the right things?
- Do you express your anger in the right way?
- How long does your anger last?
- How controlled is your anger?
- What motivates your anger?

- Is your anger "primed and ready" to respond to another person's habitual sins?
- What is the effect of your anger?

Jesus' focus was on God's glory, not his own.

To understand Jesus' anger, you must understand where the money changers were hawking their wares. The Temple building itself was not large, but the surrounding courtyards were. The complex occupied nearly 12 acres. These courtyards included the Women's Courtyard, which was surrounded by barricade that non-Jews were not allowed to pass. Beyond the barricade was the Court of the Gentiles. This was where Annas had set up the merchant's

tables. When Jesus overturned the tables, his words illuminated God's intention for the court of the Gentiles. He said, "It is written, 'My house shall be called a house of prayer' but you have made it a den of robbers."[94] Jesus was referencing the prophet Isaiah. The context of Jesus' statement offers a useful insight. Prior to his quotation from Isaiah, we read, "And *the foreigners* who join themselves to the Lord, to minister to him, to love the name of the Lord, and to be his servants..."[95] Following the quotation we read, "for my house shall be called a house of prayer for *all peoples*" [emphasis added].[96]

God's intention had been to bring glory to himself through the saving of the Gentile nations. His desire was that the Gentile courtyard be used for prayer gatherings—specifically to pray for the Gentile nations to come to know him. Not only had the religious leaders failed to do so, but they had grabbed that very real estate and used it to take advantage of the poor and needy. Both were appalling to Jesus, and he responded with intentional, well-thought out, righteous anger. In his book *The Heart Anger*, Robert Jones explains further:

> What does cultivating Godly anger involve? Refocus your heart on God and his kingdom, rights and concerns. Repent of self-centered desires. Meditate on God's actions and attributes. Passion for God is the seed bed for righteous anger. It alone produces hatred of sin.[97]

Jesus' anger is so different than my own. More often than not, my anger is about the violation of my rights, not someone else's. Likewise, I am less concerned about the glory of God than my own exaltation. I assume your struggle with anger is similar. For Jesus, though, God's glory was central, and his concern for the welfare of others was all-consuming. Like two divine fires, they stoked the righteous anger in the heart of Christ. Those fires resulted in action that sought to preserve the glory of God and protect those in need.

Avoiding Unrighteous Anger

WHILE JESUS did practice righteous anger on a few occasions, he was also able to say no to multiple temptations to give in to unrighteous anger. We tend to look to our challenging circumstances as the reason we are grow angry. Studying how Jesus prepared to face such circumstances is helpful when we face similar temptations. Here are three circumstances that Jesus faced: he didn't get what he deserved, he was falsely accused, and he suffered unjustly.

When you don't get what you think you deserve.

A cursory reading of the Gospels will reveal that Jesus didn't get what he deserved.[98] Prior to his crucifixion Jesus warns his disciples what is about to happen to him: "Let these words sink into your ears: The Son of Man is about to be delivered into the hands of men."[99] What Jesus deserves is applause, praise, and worship. What he receives is harsh treatment from those who should have known better. In the midst of such a tragedy, Jesus reveals a means to avoid unrighteous anger: humility. In the verses that follow, the disciples begin to argue about who will be the greatest. Jesus takes this opportunity to instruct them on humility.

> An argument arose among them as to which of them was the greatest. But Jesus, knowing the reasoning of their hearts, took a child and put him by his side and said to them, "Whoever receives this child in my name receives me, and whoever receives me receives him who sent me. *For he who is least among you all is the one who is great* [emphasis added]."[100]

When was the last time you heard of someone who was "humbly angry?" The words don't work well together, do they? Our unrighteous anger often flares when we don't get what we think we deserve.[101] Well-meaning friends often point out the injustice, further inciting our anger. But the person trying to walk in humility is not consumed with what he believes he has coming to him. His attentiveness on "others first" moves his focus off of himself and what he believes he deserves. This is the reason Jesus said: *For he who is least among you all is the one who is great.* The Scriptures confirm humility as a character quality that Jesus possessed. The apostle Paul wrote,

> Have this mind among yourselves, which is yours in Christ Jesus, who, though he was in the form of God, did not count equality with God a thing to be grasped, but emptied himself, by taking the form of a servant, being born in the likeness of men. And being found in human form, he humbled himself by becoming obedient to the point of death, even death on a cross.[102]

Unrighteous anger is fueled when we believe we aren't getting what we deserve. Genuine humility guards us against that sense of entitlement, thereby thwarting our sinful anger.

When you suffer unjustly.

Jesus not only predicted his suffering, he actually experienced it. He was treated unjustly and did not retaliate. He was reviled, but he did not revile in return.[103] Jesus didn't feel the need to point out the wrong done to him because he trusted his Father to make it right in the future.[104] Unrighteous anger is impatient. It wants things to be set straight immediately. When God hasn't acted on our timetable, we take matters into our own hands and grow angry.

How was Jesus able to wait so patiently on the God who judges justly, even when he was being treated unjustly? Jesus saw that suffering—even if unjust—could be purposeful. He also understood its temporary nature. Notice the last phrase of Jesus' prediction:

> The Son of Man must suffer many things and be rejected by the elders and chief priests and scribes, and be killed, and *on the third day be raised* [emphasis added].[105]

Jesus doesn't stop his prediction at his suffering, rejection and murder; he added, of all things, his resurrection. To avoid anger, Jesus only discussed his impending mistreatment in the context of its purpose and temporary nature. Angry people speak of unjust suffering as if the story ends there. They rarely place their personal suffering in the context of its purpose or brevity. Jesus did both. Elsewhere, he said:

> For whoever would save his life will lose it, but whoever loses his life for my sake will find it. For what does it profit a man if he gains the whole world and loses or forfeits himself.[106]

Jesus looked to the far-future, and he encouraged each of us to do the same. He saw a world that had yet to come. His physical life was short-lived in relation to his heavenly future. He interpreted the injustice done him in that context. Even if everyone had treated him kindly and properly—even if he gained the whole world—would it be profitable?

Jesus also understood that the redemption of mankind was resting on his shoulders.[107] His suffering was therefore purposeful. For Jesus, as well as us, this is a truth that must be accepted by faith. As a pastor, I've been in the emergency room as a father holds the lifeless body of his only son. His tears splash hard on the cold tile floor. His wife weeps uncontrollably by his side. The stark hospital lighting seems insistent on illuminating their pain for all to see.

As a caregiver, I have to acknowledge the apparent purposelessness of human suffering. Death takes one child and overlooks a hundred others. But just because we don't see suffering's purpose today doesn't mean there isn't one. This is why Paul wrote to the Romans:

> But we rejoice in our sufferings, knowing that suffering produces endurance, and endurance produces character, and character produces hope, and hope does not put us to shame, because God's love has been poured into your hearts.[108]

Hope can still exist in the midst of suffering because there comes a day when suffering will be no more. And, while we may not understand its purpose today, we must put our hope in the God who does.[109]

How to respond when you're falsely accused.

Being falsely accused is hard to take. Most false accusations don't simply deal with our actions; they usually go after our motives. That's why they tend to hurt so much. Marital conflicts often get stuck here. An action has been repeated so many times that the aggrieved spouse begins to give it intention and motive. In their accusation, they skip right over the "what" of the offense and move to the "why."

Jesus' example is masterful here. Throughout his ministry, he is falsely accused a number of times.[110] There is one occasion that must have been incredibly difficult to endure: the day the religious leaders accused him of healing by the power of Satan.

> Now he [Jesus] was casting out a demon [...] when the demon had gone out, the mute man spoke, and the people marveled. But some of them said, "He casts out demons by Beelzebul, the prince of demons," [...] But he [Jesus], knowing their thoughts, said to them, "Every kingdom divided against itself is laid waste, and a divided household falls. And if Satan also is divided against himself, how will his kingdom stand?[111]

No human being had ever known the evil intentions of Satan like Jesus. He had been directly tempted by the evil one and not fallen.[112] He had lived among the abused and addicted and seen Satan's careless destruction first hand.[113] He had sent Satan's mercenaries running every time he spoke.[114] To be accused of operating in Satan's name and using his power raises false accusations to another level. Jesus doesn't respond in anger, however. He asks two questions: one logical and one personal.

> "A divided household falls. And if Satan also is divided, how will his kingdom stand? [...] And if I cast out demons by Beelzebul [prince of demons], by whom do your sons cast them out?[115]

Remarkably, there is no expression of anger, even though he has been falsely accused. The answer to Jesus' victory over the temptation to become angry when falsely accused is found in his commitment to prayer. Luke writes his most significant commentary on Jesus' prayer life in the verses proceeding the religious leaders' accusation.

> Now Jesus was praying in a certain place, and when he finished, one of his disciples said to him, "Lord, teach us to pray [...] And he said to them [...] ask, and it will

be given to you; seek, and you will find; knock, and it will be opened to you. For everyone who asks receives, and the one who seeks finds, and to the one who knocks it will be opened.[116]

A robust prayer life was Jesus' preparation to handle false accusations without an angry response. If only we would hold our prayer time with God at the priority level that Jesus did. Our focus would be on what we say to God, not what was said about us.

When we don't get what we think we deserve we should humble ourselves. When we face suffering, we should remember it's temporary and purposeful. And when we are falsely accused, we should pray. Those are the ways that Jesus avoided unrighteous anger. If they worked for him, perhaps we should try them ourselves.

LIVE BY THE SPIRIT
How the Fruit of the Spirit Prevents Anger

ON MORE THAN one occasion I have thought that my cell phone was plugged in and charging, only to discover that its power was nearly depleted when I needed it. The power was available, but a loose connection was responsible for its inability to charge. My phone only appeared to be plugged in to the power source. I find a similar problem with many Christians. The power to be victorious over habitual sins like anger is available, but when they're tempted, they're powerless to overcome their angry responses.

In Galatians 5, the apostle Paul gives four commands that enable us to access the Holy Spirit's power. He says: walk by the Spirit, be led by the Spirit, live by the Spirit and keep in step with the Spirit.[117] In the verses between these commands, we find two lists that teach us how to access the Holy Spirit's power. The first enumerates the desires of the flesh, and the second the fruit of the Spirit. We should embrace the latter while avoiding the former.

List 1: The desires of the flesh

> Now the works of the flesh are evident: sexual immorality, impurity, sensuality, idolatry, sorcery, enmity, strife, jealousy, fits of anger, rivalries, dissensions, divisions, envy, drunkenness, orgies, and things like these.[118]

List 2: The fruit of the Spirit

> But the fruit of the Spirit is love, joy, peace, patience, kindness, goodness, faithfulness, gentleness, self-control; against such things there is no law.[119]

There are no fewer than eight words related to anger in the first list. The secret for victory over these sinful responses is found in the second list. Within the fruit of the Spirit, there are multiple replacements for the various forms of anger. To walk in the Spirit, we simply choose values from the fruit of the Spirit list to replace the angry desires that stir up within us. Then, as opposed to giving into the desires, we concentrate on practicing the replacement from the fruit of the Spirit list.

Defining the fruit of the Spirit

The following are working definitions of each of those qualities that make up the fruit of the Spirit. I recommend that you choose a few of them, memorize the definition, and then look for opportunities to apply them in environments that typically arouse your anger. Don't be quick to choose your old habit of sinful anger; instead, choose and apply the quality from this list that best fits the situation.

- **Love** is a sacrificial choice of words accompanied by actions regardless of attraction or response generated by God, not by oneself.
- **Joy** is a predetermined attitude of praise for God's goodness by maintaining an eternal focus in the midst of difficulty.
- **Peace** is a settled confidence of mind from a right relationship with God, unaffected by circumstantial change.

- **Patience** is a learned attitude revealed through a joyful willingness to remain under difficulty in order to learn God's lessons.
- **Kindness** is a tender spirit, purposefully expressed and sacrificially given, especially to the undeserving.
- **Goodness** is a focused resolve that drives us to become actively involved in the life of another, consistently expressed through generosity.
- **Faithfulness** is a promise to keep one's word and do one's best with a servant-attitude focused on the Master's approval.
- **Gentleness** is an attitude of humility, stirred by a grateful spirit and revealed in a tenderness to others, sustained by a growing trust in God.
- **Self-control** is the growing realization that one's desire to please self was crucified with Christ and replaced with a desire to glorify God.

Practicing the fruit of the Spirit

An old Chinese proverb reads: *Tell me, and I forget; show me, and I may remember; involve me, and I will understand.* The apostle Paul gave the same advice when he wrote to the Philippians, "What you have learned and received and heard and *seen in me—practice these things*, and the God of peace will be with you [emphasis added]."[120] Most of us retain a truth far better if we can visualize it rather than simply hearing it. That is why I encourage people who are trying to develop the fruit of the Spirit to think of someone who exemplifies those qualities and emulate them. In that way they are following Paul's pattern: *what you have seen in me, practice*. Ask yourself how your mentor would have responded to a situation with love, patience, or kindness. There are nine qualities that make up the fruit of the Spirit. Try finding nine people from your past that exemplify each quality. If you don't know of someone personally, than make it your goal to develop relationships with people who have made it a habit to practice the fruit of the Spirit in their lives. I have found that people living out these qualities are open to share them. In their humility they may be reticent at first, but open-ended questions will often illicit their advice.

Replacing angry desires

Once you've defined the new values and seen them exemplified in another believer, you're ready to replace the angry desires with the fruit of the Spirit qualities. Perhaps you struggle with strife, jealousy, fits of anger, rivalries, dissensions, divisions, or envy—negative qualities from list one. Prayerfully consider what qualities from list two would be the best replacement. You may wish to replace fits of anger with self-control, strife with kindness, or jealousy with love. The apostle Paul charged us with bringing every thought captive, in obedience to Christ.[121] Replacing the desires of the flesh with the fruit of the Spirit is the practical way this is done. Adding a mentor to emulate will make your spiritual growth even more productive.

How the Armor of God Protects from Anger

BECAUSE WE tend to experience anger emotionally, we forget that it must be battled spiritually. Notice Paul's reminder in the epistle of Ephesians: "Do not let the sun go down on your anger, and give no opportunity to the devil."[122] Anger, improperly dealt with, gives the spiritual forces of darkness[123] a window of influence. If we are to be victorious in spiritual realms, we must learn to use spiritual means.[124] The armor of God is essential for our spiritual protection.

Three times in the 6th chapter of Ephesians we are told to "stand against" the schemes of the devil.[125] One of Satan's schemes is for us to believe that unleashing our anger will have a positive impact. Often, we believe we are more convincing when we're angry. Yet James was explicit: *the anger of man does not accomplish the righteousness of God.*[126] Our anger does not make us more convincing, it makes us less so: because when we are angry, we often act foolishly.[127] Bitterness is another of Satan's schemes. The bitter-hearted person believes they are bringing justice to the offender by denying them forgiveness. Yet the offender may not even be aware of the hurt they caused. To the offended, it feels like they are hurting the offender simply because they are bitter. These are Satan's schemes, and because our anger feels so justified, we assume they are truthful. God's Word arms us to be ready for such battles.

> Stand therefore, having fastened on the belt of truth, and having put on the breastplate of righteousness, and, as shoes for your feet, having put on the readiness

given by the gospel of peace. In all circumstances take up the shield of faith, with which you can extinguish all the flaming darts of the evil one; and take the helmet of salvation, and the sword of the Spirit, which is the word of God.[128]

Belt of truth

During biblical times, a warrior would tuck the loose ends of his robe up into his belt. This would give him greater freedom in fighting; allowing him both balance and quickness. Often, this might be the difference between life and death. Satan's mode of operation is deceit.[129] Because anger is a feeling-based sin, we would expect our emotions to be the vehicle that he would use to tempt us deceitfully. Truth counters deceit. This is why we must review the truth of God's Word repeatedly. When you do this you are reaffirming the truth and weakening the influence of Satan's deceitful ways in your life. To aid you in this process, I have provided over 150 biblical passages in the form of "replacement lists" to overcome the various forms of anger (see pages 66-68 for the Bible references).

Breastplate of righteousness

The soldier's breastplate protected his vital organs. It was made of a combination of metal and leather so the enemy's blows would glance off and not penetrate. The armor did have openings providing for the movement of the body in battle. These openings were potentially dangerous. Theologian Wayne Grudem makes this spiritual application:

> Nevertheless, we should recognize that sinning (even by Christians) does give a foothold for some kind of

demonic influence in our lives. Thus Paul could say, "Be angry but do not sin; do not let the sun go down on your anger, and give no opportunity to the devil" (Eph. 4:26). Wrongful anger apparently can give opportunity for the devil (or demons) to exert some kind of negative influence in our lives—perhaps by attacking us through our emotions and perhaps by increasing the wrongful anger that we already feel against others. Similarly, Paul mentions "the breastplate of righteousness" (Eph. 6:14) as part of the armor that we are to use standing against "the wiles of the devil" and in contending "against the principalities, against the powers, against the world rulers of this present darkness, against the spiritual hosts of wickedness in the heavenly places" (Eph. 6:11–12). If we have areas of continuing sin in our lives, then there are weaknesses and holes in our "breastplate of righteousness," and these are areas in which we are vulnerable to demonic attack.[130]

Grudem's comments serve as a vivid reminder that we're in a battle. We dare not take a few failures with anger lightly. When those failures are never dealt with, they provide holes in the armor that leave us weakened for the next attack. Only Christ was fully righteous. As we dwell upon his righteousness, it inspires us to live righteously too.

Gospel Shoes

Meditating on the gospel is essential if we are to be ready to share it when the opportunity arises. But dwelling on the Gospel accomplishes far more than preparing us to witness. In his excellent book *The Gospel Primer*, Milton

Vincent makes this point:
> God did not give us His gospel just so we could embrace it and be converted. Actually, He offers it to us every day as a gift that keeps on giving to us everything we need for life and godliness. The wise believer learns this truth early and becomes proficient in extracting available benefits from the gospel each day. We extract these benefits by being absorbed in the gospel, speaking it to ourselves when necessary, and by daring to reckon it true in all we do.[131]

It's hard to be overcome with sinful anger when you are dwelling on the gracious gospel truth that Jesus willingly went to the cross in your place. As we meditate on the gospel message, it weakens our sense of entitlement. You can't be overcome with anger for another when you are overcome with God's grace towards you.

Shield of faith

The soldier's shield was large (2.5 x 4.5 feet). It was meant to protect the whole body. Covered with oiled leather, it could extinguish the fiery darts of the enemy.[132] Our protection against the temptations of Satan is the shield of faith. This describes our confidence in God's Word and his promises. It's difficult to sink in to a sense of entitlement and anger (see the downward staircase, page 27) when you are constantly reviewing the promises of God. Satan's temptations can't reach the heart when the shield of faith is in place (Reviewing the "Promises about God and the Gospel" is an excellent way to strengthen your shield of faith, page 71).

Helmet of salvation

Keeping an eternal perspective on the benefits of our salvation is a good deterrent to anger. Max Anders comments,

> First Thessalonians speaks of the helmet of the "hope of salvation," which is probably a parallel idea [to the helmet of salvation in Ephesians 6:17]. That being the case, taking the helmet of salvation could be understood as resting our hope in the future and living in this world according to the value system of the next.[133]

Making priority and value judgments with one eye on eternity helps us overcome the narrow focus on our unmet desires. James spoke of those unmet desires being the fuel for angry reactions.[134]

Sword of the Spirit

This metaphor for the Word of God is a descriptive reminder we are in a spiritual battle. Those battling various temptations (including anger) are sure to face frustration unless they have memorized key Scriptures and are adept at using them when temptation comes. Chuck Swindoll says that Scripture memory is the most underused spiritual resource of today's Christian. Don Whitney makes the same case when he writes,

> The Word of God is the "sword of the Spirit," but the Holy Spirit cannot give you a weapon you have not stored in the armory of your mind. Imagine yourself in the midst of a decision and needing guidance, or struggling with a difficult temptation and needing victory. The Holy Spirit rushes to your mental arsenal, flings open the door, but all He finds is a John 3:16, a Genesis 1:1, and a Great Commission. Those are great swords,

but they're not made for every battle.[135]

The idea that we need to have the right sword for the right battle is a distinctive of the Biblical Strategies resources. I believe that we remember Scripture best when we learn the verses that will help us at our point of need. This provides instant application of the text to our temptation or struggle. That doesn't mean we simply learn verses about our sins. Rather, we ought to memorize from both a defensive and offensive posture. To play good defense, we memorize verses in the lie/truth formula, as this exposes temptation's deception. To play good offense, we memorize verses about the character of God and the nature of the gospel, as this weakens temptation's appeal (see pages 70-71).

Suiting up with the proper spiritual armor is God's protection against our temptation to succumb to sinful anger. I recently had a friend share with me his experience in "Survival School" for the US military. His team was dropped three-days-deep in the wilderness—without food or water—and required to find their way out. He told me he was flipped upside down in a submerged tank that was meant to simulate a sunken helicopter. While I was trying to imagine the panic of that experience, he mentioned the hardest part: he had to escape the underwater challenge blindfolded. Survival School prepared him for near-death encounters by placing him in the most difficult of circumstances.

Perhaps we would be more victorious in our battle with anger if we took our preparation that seriously. Anger is a spiritual battle. It's time to suit up in your spiritual armor and become proficient with the Sword of the Spirit.

Extinguishing the Fire

OVER THE last several years three houses in our neighborhood have burned to the ground. Fortunately there was no loss of life in the fires, but the damage to homes and belongings surpassed a million dollars. The causes of each fire were unique: the first was caused by a family pet, the second was a result of an appliance failure, the third fell to a lightening strike. While the homes were as different as the causes of the fires, they each had at least one thing in common: there was no one home when the fire started. The smoke detectors screeched their warnings to empty rooms. What could have easily been extinguished in the beginning stages turned into three infernos that lit up the night sky.

When you feel anger's fire start to burn, reach quickly for one of the extinguishers. Take forgiveness over bitterness. Seize patience instead of wrath. Express love over anger. Choose thoughtful listening in lieu of clamor. Reach for grace and truth instead of slander. Do kind deeds as opposed to malicious ones. These replacements are like a divine repression system. They extinguish the fire early before it's had a chance to inflict further damage.

Ignoring the angry feelings stirring in your heart is like starting a fire in your house and locking the door on the way out. You must consistently choose the proper replacement, and the earlier the better. In the following pages you will find over 150 scriptures that were selected as the essential replacements for the various forms of anger. As you take them to heart, you will find hope for change.

For years my family has enjoyed an annual vacation in

the Colorado Rockies. We were scheduled for that vacation a decade ago, the summer the Hayman fire erupted. The following summer we rode horses through the charred remains of the forest. The blackened trees stood like tombstones, poignant reminders of what one match can do. Even though a year had passed since the fire, our clothes would reek of smoke when we returned from our trail ride, our faces blackened from the ash-filled dust. As the years progressed, however, the landscape changed. First came the mountain grasses, insistent on pushing through the rocky soil. Then, the deep purple and bright yellow wild flowers filled in the landscape. Plants appeared that could have never grown in the shade of those hundred-year-old pines. Aspen groves sprouted out of nowhere; their silvery leaves whispering in the mountain breezes. In place of the fire's destruction, vibrant life sprang forth. Even the dead Ponderosa Pines shed their blackened bark, saying farewell to the final residue of the fire.

Likewise, there is hope of new life for the angry person. As you choose forgiveness, love, and patience, you will leave anger's destruction behind. There are great opportunities for new growth in the days ahead. Don't be discouraged by an occasional flare up. Just keep applying the key replacements to your angry ways. God will cause new growth to spring forth where once there was death and destruction.

Let everyone be quick to listen, slow to speak, and slow to become angry. For the anger of man does not accomplish the righteousness of God.
James 1:19-20

How to Apply What You've Learned

The discovery of new truths is the beginning—but discovery by itself cannot accomplish real change. To do that, you will need to replace your old habits with new ones, your old ideas with more accurate ones, and your old thoughts with more biblical ones. The final pages of this booklet are dedicated to helping you establish those new habits. Prayer, Scripture, and the Holy Spirit were the divine resources that Jesus used, and those same resources are available to you and me today.

(1) Prayer

Whatever the struggle, we have a tendency to see prayer as a panic button—we hit it only when we're in need. Yet, the Bible has over 650 examples of prayer. These are an excellent resource for growth in your prayer life. The following pages offer two different prayer patterns and a listing of the names and attributes of God.

(2) Scripture

A growing understanding of and confidence in God is essential to overcoming anger. Three attributes of God are particularly worth noting: his forgiveness, patience, and love. I have provided 28 days of Bible readings in these areas. You will also find 150 key replacement passages. To aid with Scripture retrieval, I have included 20 biblical passages to memorize that apply directly to anger.

(3) The Spirit

Dependence on the Spirit is essential for overcoming anger. Developing new habits by walking in the Spirit is the means through which we express that daily dependence. The "3 Circles of Responsibility" is a graphic that describes God's part and our part in bringing about change.

The 10 Minute Prayer Pattern: PRAY

The *PRAY* acrostic is a memory device for prayer. It can be as short as a few minutes, or may include more time as God leads. PRAY stands for **P**raise, **R**epent, **A**sk, and **Y**ield.

(1) Praise

At the beginning of prayer, praise the *who*, *what*, and *why* of God. Remember *who* he is by reflecting upon his character. When you remember *what* he's done, you are meditating on his works. Finally, remember the *why* of God. He is motivated by his steadfast love towards us (Psa. 100:5).

(2) Repent

Once you've thought about what God has done, you can move easily to what *you* haven't done. Repentance takes place when we remember our failures and turn from them. A humble confession in prayer reveals a dependence on the Spirit in order to be restored to God. True repentance includes my actions and attitudes (Phil. 2:5).

(3) Ask

Jesus taught us to *ask* of God, and Paul gave us a great prayer list to follow (see Col. 1:9-12). The spiritual nature of the prayers of Scriptures are helpful in praying for yourself and others.

(4) Yield

Jesus grew to the point where he could say, "Not my will but yours be done." Yielding your desires (as hard as that may initially be) is an essential element of prayer. Once you've made known your requests, make sure you surrender your desires.

Habakkuk's Prayer

The prophet Habakkuk was angry and confused. He knew his own country had problems, but their wicked deeds paled in comparison to the Chaldeans. His anger is revealed through a series of questions he asked God. Then, as he affirms God's greatness and power, his angry questions turn to quiet trust. The book bearing his name provides an excellent prayer pattern for the person struggling with anger.

(1) Ask God your questions honestly(1:1-4; 12-17)

Habakkuk asks six questions in the first chapter of his book. These questions surface because the evil he sees in the world seems inconsistent with the God he believes in. Notice that Habakkuk doesn't blame God, he *asks* him. A note in *The Nelson Study Bible* gives God's response:

> God did not strike Habakkuk down for these questions. He answered. The Lord himself will establish his kingdom. He will hold all people and nations accountable.[136]

God is not opposed to our questions when they come from a heart that is genuinely seeking answers. Habakkuk's example is one to emulate. Don't simply stew in your anger; bring your honest questions to God in prayer.

(2) Reject any known idols(2:18-20)

Anger can grow when we don't get what we want. The Bible defines those unmet desires as idols. Habakkuk acknowledges the futility of these unmet desires (idols) prior to his prayer of trust in chapter 3. This is an important step in the prayer life of an angry person. Consider: *what desires are not being met, and why do you feel so justi-*

fied in your anger about them? Once you've pinpointed your idols, take steps towards repentance. Acknowledge where you were wrong in assuming that an idol could satisfy. Turn back again to God in worship. He alone can satisfy.

(3) Review the character of God (3:2-16)

Habakkuk's prayer in chapter 3 is filled with references to God's character and his power. The more that we meditate on God's character (see pages 63-65), the less likely we are to develop a discontented spirit that erupts in anger. When you dwell upon the character of God instead of your painful circumstances, you will discover that your trust in God will increase and you faith will be strengthened.

(4) Reaffirm your trust in God (3:17-19)

Habakkuk concludes his prayer with one of the most confident assertions of God's trustworthiness found in the Scriptures:

> Though the fig tree should not blossom,
> > nor fruit be on the vines,
> the produce of the olive fail
> > and the fields yield no food,
> the flock be cut off from the fold
> > and there be no herd in the stalls,
> yet I will rejoice in the Lord;
> > I will take joy in the God of my salvation.
> God, the Lord, is my strength;
> > he makes my feet like the deer's;
> > he makes me tread on my high places.[137]

When you're struggling with anger, take your burdens to the Lord: (1) ask God your questions honestly, (2) reject any known idols, (3) review the character of God, and (4) reaffirm your trust in God.

30 Days of Praying the Attributes of God

The following list was developed by the Navigators. A 30-day calendar style listing of these names and attributes is available at their website: www.navigators.org under the tools tab. Reflecting on one of God's attributes each day is a helpful means to recognize his control in areas where we do not have control.

1 God is Jehovah. The name of the independent, self-complete being—"I AM WHO I AM"—only belongs to Jehovah God. Our proper response to Him is to fall down in fear and awe of the One who possesses all authority (Ex. 3:13-15).

2 God is Jehovah-M'Kaddesh. This name means "the God who sanctifies." A God separate from all that is evil requires that the people who follow Him be cleansed from all evil (Lev. 20:7,8).

3 God is infinite. God is beyond measurement—we cannot define Him by size or amount. He has no beginning, no end, and no limits (Ro. 11:33).

4 God is omnipotent. This means God is all-powerful. He spoke all things into being, and all things—every cell, every breath, every thought—are sustained by Him. There is nothing too difficult for Him to do (Jer. 32:17,18, 26,27).

5 God is good. God is the embodiment of perfect goodness, He is kind, benevolent, and full of good will toward all creation (Ps. 119:65-72).

6 God is love. God's love is so great that He gave His only Son to bring us into fellowship with Him. God's love not only encompasses the world, but embraces each of us personally and intimately (1 Jn. 4:7-10).

7 God is Jehovah-jireh. "The God who provides." Just as He provided yesterday, He will also provide today and tomorrow. He grants deliverance from sin, the oil of joy for the ashes of sorrow, and citizenship in His Kingdom for all those adopted into His household (Gen. 22:9-14).

8 God is Jehovah-shalom. "The God of peace." We are meant to know the fullness of God's perfect peace, or His "shalom." God's peace surpasses understanding and sustains us even through difficult times. It is the product of fully being what we were created to be (Jud. 6:16-24).

9 God is immutable. All that God is, He has always been. All that He has been and is, He will ever be. He is ever perfect and unchanging (Ps. 102:25-28).

Suggestions for prayer: names & attributes of God

10 God is transcendent. We must not think of God as simply the highest in an order of beings. This would be to grant Him eminence, but he is more than eminent. He is transcendent—existing beyond and above the created universe (Ps. 113:4,5).

11 God is just. God is righteous and holy, fair, and equitable in all things. We can trust Him to always do what is right (Ps. 75:1-7).

12 God is holy. God's holiness is not simply a better version of the best we know. God is utterly and supremely untainted. His holiness stands apart—unique and incomprehensible (Rev. 4:8-11).

13 God is Jehovah-rophe. This name means "Jehovah heals." God alone provides the remedy for mankind's brokenness through His son, Jesus Christ. The Gospel is the physical, moral, and spiritual remedy for all people (Ex. 15:22-26).

15 God is omniscient. This means God is all-knowing. God's knowledge encompasses every possible thing that exists, has ever existed, or will ever exist. Nothing is a mystery to Him (Ps. 139:1-6).

16 God is omnipresent. God is everywhere—in and around everything, close to everyone. "'Do not I fill heaven and earth?' declares the Lord" (Ps. 139:7-12).

17 God is merciful. God's merciful compassion is infinite and inexhaustible. Through Christ, He took the judgment that was rightfully ours and placed it on His own shoulders. He [...] works for all people to turn to Him and to live under His justification (Deu. 4:29-31).

18 God is sovereign. God presides over every event, great or small, and He is in control of our lives. To be sovereign, He must be all-knowing and all-powerful, and by His sovereignty He rules His entire creation (1 Chr. 29:11-13).

19 God is Jehovah-nissi. This name means "God our banner." Under His banner we go from triumph to triumph and say, "Thanks be to God, who gives us the victory through our Lord Jesus Christ" (1 Cor. 15:57; Ex. 17:8-15).

20 God is wise. All God's acts are accomplished through His infinite wisdom. He always acts for our good, to conform us to Christ. Our good and His glory are inextricably bound together (Pro. 3:19,20).

21 God is faithful. Out of His faithfulness God honors His covenants and fulfills His promises. Our hope for the future rests upon God's faithfulness (Psa. 89:1-8)

22 God is wrathful. Unlike human anger, God's wrath is never capricious, self-indulgent, or irritable. It is the right and necessary reaction to objective moral evil (Nah. 1:2-8)

23 God is full of grace. Grace is God's good pleasure that moves Him to grant merit where it is undeserved and to forgive debt that cannot be repaid (Eph. 1:5-8).

24 God is our Comforter. Jesus called the Holy Spirit the "Comforter," and the apostle Paul writes that the Lord is "the God of all comfort" (2 Cor. 1:3,4).

25 God is El-Shaddai. This name means "God Almighty,"the God who is all-sufficient and all-bountiful, the source of all blessings (Gen. 49:22-26).

26 God is Father. Jesus taught us to pray, "Our Father" (Matthew 6:9), and the Spirit of God taught us to cry, "Abba, Father.," an intimate Aramaic term similar to "Daddy." The Creator [...] cares for each one of us as if we were the only child He had (Rom. 8:15-17).

27 God is the Church's head. God the Son, Jesus, is the head of the Church. As the head, the part of the body that sees, hears, thinks, and decides, He gives the orders that [...] the body lives by (Eph. 1:22,23).

28 God is our intercessor. Knowing our temptations, God the Son intercedes for us. He opens the doors for us to boldly ask God the Father for mercy. Thus, God is both the initiation and conclusion of true prayer (Heb. 4:14-16).

29 God is Adonai. This name means "Master" or "Lord." God, our Adonai, calls all God's people to acknowledge themselves as His servants, claiming His right to reign as Lord of our lives (2 Sam. 7:18-20).

30 God is Elohim. This name means "Strength" or "Power." He is transcendent, mighty and strong. Elohim is the great name of God, displaying His supreme power, sovereignty, and faithfulness in His covenant relationship with us (Gen. 17:7,8).

Taken from The Navigators website[138]

Suggestions for reading: key replacement passages

Key Replacement Passages

The following passages are offered for your further study. Choose the type of anger with which you struggle and then review the biblical passages in that replacement column. Tab the page in your Bible, then highlight the verse for quick reference; or consider writing your favorite passages on 3x5 cards for easy access.

Replace bitterness with **forgiveness**	Replace wrath with **patience**
1 Kings 8:46-48	Psalm 37:7-9
Psalm 32	Psalm 40:1
Psalm 51	Psalm 130:5
Psalm 103:10-14	Proverbs 15:18
Psalm 130:3	Ecclesiastes 7:8,9
Proverbs 10:12	Isaiah 4:31
Proverbs 17:9	Jeremiah 29:11
Proverbs 25:21	Lamentations 3:26
Ecclesiastes 7:20	Romans 5:3-5
Jeremiah 31:34	Romans 8:25
Micah 7:18-20	Romans 12:12
Matthew 6:14-15	Romans 15:4, 5
Matthew 18:21-22	1 Corinthians 13:4
Matthew 26:28	Galatians 5:22
Mark 11:25	Galatians 6:9
Luke 6:27, 37	Ephesians 4:2
Luke 7:36-50	Colossians 1:11
Luke 17:1-11	Colossians 3:12
Acts 2:38	1 Thessalonians 1:3
Romans 12:20	1 Thessalonians 5:14
Ephesians 2:8-9	2 Timothy 2:24
Ephesians 4:32	Hebrews 6:12, 15
Philippians 3:13-14	Hebrews 10:3-37
Colossians 3:13	James 1:3, 4
Philemon	James 1:19-20
1 John 1:9	1 Peter 2:19-23

Suggestions for reading: key replacement passages

Replace anger with **Love**	Replace clamor with **thoughtful listening**
Deuteronomy 6:5	Exodus 7:13
Deuteronomy 10:19	2 Kings 17:14
Deuteronomy 15:7-8	Nehemiah 9:17
Deuteronomy 30:6	Ezekiel 12:2
Jeremiah 31:3	Jeremiah 6:10
Psalm 18:1-4	Jeremiah 7:13
Psalm 103:8, 17	Jeremiah 13:17
Psalm 136:126	Jeremiah 26:3-6
Proverbs 3:12	Jeremiah 29:19
Proverbs 17:9, 17	Jeremiah 32:33
Matthew 22:37-39	Jeremiah 35:15
Matthew 25:35	Zechariah 7:11-12
Luke 10:29-37	Psalm 58:4
John 3:16-17	Proverbs 2:2
John 10:17	Proverbs 8:32-34
John 13:1, 34-36	Proverbs 12:15
John 14:23	Proverbs 18:13
John 15:9-13, 17	Proverbs 19:20, 27
John 17:24	Proverbs 20:12
John 21:15-17	Proverbs 25:12
Romans 5:8	Matthew 7:24-27
1 Corinthians 13:4-7	Matthew 11:15
2 Corinthians 2:4	Matthew 18:15-17
Galatians 5:13, 14	Mark 4:1-20
Ephesians 3:17-19	Mark 9:7
Ephesians 4:2	Luke 10:39
1 Thessalonians 1:3	John 8:47
1 Timothy 1:5	John 10:27
1 Timothy 4:12	Acts 28:27
Hebrews 12:6	1 Thessalonians 2:13
1 Peter 1:22	2 Timothy 4:3-4
1 Peter 4:8	Hebrews 5:11
1 John 3:14-18	James 1:19-20; 22-24
1 John 4:7-11, 16, 21	James 5:16

Suggestions for reading: key replacement passages

Replace slander with **grace and truth**	Replace malice with **kind deeds**
2 Samuel 9:1-7 (grace)	2 Samuel 9:1-13
Psalm 15:2 (truth)	Nehemiah 9:17
Psalm 19:7-14 (truth)	Isaiah 54:10
Psalm 37:25-26 (grace)	Micah 6:8
Psalm 51:6 (truth)	Nahum 1:7
Psalm 117:2 (grace, truth)	Zechariah 7:9-10
Psalm 119:89, 152, 160 (truth)	Zephaniah 3:17
Proverbs 8:7 (truth)	Psalm 112:5
Proverbs 12:17 (truth)	Proverbs 3:2-4; 27-28
Zechariah 8:16 (truth)	Proverbs 11:17
Matthew 18:23-35 (grace)	Matthew 5:16; 43-48
Mark 13:31 (grace)	Matthew 25:34-36
John 4:23 (truth)	Mark 8:34-37
John 8:13-18, 32 (truth)	Luke 6:35
John 1:14-18 (grace, truth)	Luke 10:25-37
John 14:6 (truth)	Luke 12:33-34
John 17:17 (truth)	Luke 16:19-31
Romans 5:2 (grace)	John 13:35
1 Corinthians 2:1-5 (grace)	Romans 2:13
1 Corinthians 15:10 (grace)	Romans 11:22
2 Corinthians 4:2 (truth)	Galatians 5:14
2 Corinthians 12:8-9 (grace)	Galatians 6:9-10
Ephesians 4:15 (grace, truth)	Ephesians 4:32
Ephesians 4:25 (truth)	Colossians 3:23-25
Colossians 1:3-6 (grace)	1 Timothy 6:17-19
Colossians 4:6 (grace)	2 Timothy 1:16-18
2 Timothy 2:25 (truth)	Titus 3:4-7
Titus 2:11-14 (grace)	Hebrews 6:10-12
Hebrews 4:16 (grace)	Hebrews 10:24
Hebrews 5:2 (grace)	James 1:27
1 Peter 1:25 (truth)	James 2:14-17
1 Peter 4:10 (grace)	1 Peter 3:8-9
1 Peter 5:5, 10 (grace)	2 Peter 1:5-7
1 John 1:6 (truth)	1 John 4:20-21

28 Daily Bible Readings for Anger

These readings focus on three of the six replacement values for anger—forgiveness, patience and love.

DAILY READINGS

DAILY APPLICATION

Forgiveness

Day 1: Psalm 32:1-11
Day 2: Luke 7:36-50
Day 3: Ephesians 2:1-9
Day 4: Psalm 103:1-22
Day 5: Luke 17:1-11
Day 6: Philemon 1-25
Day 7: Psalm 51
Day 8: Matthew 18:15-22
Day 9: Matthew 18:23-35

As you read these Bible passages consider: (1) How is forgiveness expressed in this passage? (2) For what kind of wrongs has God forgiven you? (3) Are there those from whom you have withheld forgiveness and given bitterness a foothold?

Patience

Day 10: Pro. 15:18; 19:11; 25:15
Day 11: James 1:16-21
Day 12: 2 Peter 3:8-13
Day 13: Romans 15:4-7
Day 14: Hebrews 6:9-20
Day 15: Psalm 37:1-11
Day 16: Hebrews 12:3-11
Day 17: Ecclesiastes 7:5-14
Day 18: James 5:7-8

As you read these Bible passages consider: (1) What are some of the benefits that are promised to the patient person? (2) In what ways has God been patient with you?

Love

Day 19: Pro. 3:12; 17:9, 17
Day 20: Luke 10:29-37
Day 21: 2 Samuel 9:1-13
Day 22: 1 Cor. 13
Day 23: 1 John 4:7-11, 16, 21
Day 24: John 13:1, 34-36
Day 25: Luke 10:25-37
Day 26: John 21:15-17
Day 27: 1 John 3:14-18
Day 28: Matthew 22:37-39

As you read these Bible passages consider: (1) How is God's love revealed in this passage? (2) What should be my response to God's love (3) What steps can I take to love others better?

Suggestions for Scripture retrieval: defense & offense

The Scripture Retrieval Method

The Scripture retrieval method is based upon three premises: (1) Scripture provides an excellent *defense* against temptation. This is why the first ten verses listed below are learned in the lie/truth formula to defend against temptation. (2) Scripture provides an excellent *offense* to weaken temptation's appeal. This is why the second ten verses are learned about the character of God and the nature of the Gospel. Loving God well and appreciating the Gospel weakens the draw of temptation. (3) We learn the Scriptures best when we *understand* the words we are memorizing and *apply* them to our real life challenges. For this reason, memory alone is an ineffective means of defending against sin.

Biblical Truths to Combat the Deceiver's Lies

Lie 1: When you respond in anger, others are more likely to change. Truth: James 1:19-20

Lie 2: When you respond in anger, others will take you seriously. Truth: Proverbs 14:29, GWT

Lie 3: You keep falling. You'll never have victory over your anger. Truth: Philippians 1:6; 4:13

Lie 4: If you put off dealing with your anger, it will be better tomorrow. Truth: Ephesians 4:26-27

Lie 5: You can't change—that's just the way you are. Truth: 2 Corinthians 5:17

Lie 6: Being angry is how you show others you're strong. Truth: Proverbs 16:32

Lie 7: You are right to react with anger; others hurt you. Truth: Romans 12:19

Lie 8: Your difficult circumstances make you angry. Truth: Philippians 4:11-12

Lie 9: You don't have a choice but to get angry. It just happens. Truth: Romans 6:16

Lie 10: You were mistreated and misjudged—you have a right to be angry. Truth: 1 Peter 2:21, 23

Biblical Promises about God and the Gospel

Promise 1: God's protection is perfect.
   Passage: Psalm 18:30; Nahum 1:7

Promise 2: God loves me and enjoys acting on my behalf.
   Passage: Zephaniah 3:17

Promise 3: God saved me when I was helpless.
   Truth: Colossians 2:13-14

Promise 4: Nothing can separate me from the love of God.
   Passage: Romans 8:35, 37

Promise 5: God is patient with the undeserving.
   Passage: 2 Peter 3:8-9

Promise 6: God is sovereign over all.
   Passage: Daniel 4:34-35

Promise 7: God will strengthen me when I am weak.
   Passage: Isaiah 41:10, 13

Promise 8: God is gracious with my failures.
   Passage: 1 Corinthians 15:10

Promise 9: Nothing is too difficult for God.
   Passage: Jeremiah 32:27

Promise 10: God is trustworthy.
   Passage: Psalm 25:14-15

Visit biblicalstrategies.com to order these 20 memory verse cards with helpful commentary on the back of each card.

3 Circles of Responsibility

In our interaction with others, it is easy to grow angry when they are not doing what we think would be best for them. Even if our motive is right, we are tempted to manipulate them through an angry response. For instance, we desire to help the friend who has a drug addiction, or the person involved in an abusive relationship. But how should we respond when they disregard our advice? That's when our unrighteous anger will often reveal it self. Fortunately, there is a passage in 2 Timothy that qualifies your responsibility and releases you from the tendency towards anger and manipulation.

Servant	And the Lord's servant must not be quarrelsome but kind to everyone, able to teach, patiently enduring evil, correcting his opponents with gentleness (2 Tim. 2:24-25a).
Holy Spirit	God may perhaps grant them repentance leading to a knowledge of the truth (2 Tim. 2:25b)
Opponent	and they may come to their senses and escape from the snare of the devil, after being captured by him to do his will (2 Tim. 2:26)

The three circles represent the three participants found in this passage. The circle labeled "servant" represents you and your responses to the one who is in opposition. Verses 24 and 25 give five reminders for how we should respond. The second circle corresponds to God and his role in a broken relationship. The final circle denotes the one who is in opposition. We'll call him the opponent. Verse 26 gives his challenging spiritual condition: he is a captive. It's easy to envision the family member addicted to illegal drugs or the teenager insistent upon disobeying their parents as a "captive." Their actions often reflect their refusal to take responsibility for their choices. When they don't take responsibility for their wrongdoing and blame others for their choices, it's easy to respond in anger. Parents are especially prone to this type of response: we believe that the angrier our response, the more likely we are to convince our children of their need to change. James gives us a sharp warning that this is not the case:

> Know this my beloved brothers: let everyone be quick to hear, slow to speak, slow to anger; for the anger of man does not produce the righteousness of God.[139]

The passage in 2 Timothy compliments James' warning by reminding each of us how we ought to respond to others when we're tempted to be angry. The circles below reflect a proper biblical paradigm. Rather than manipulate our opponent through anger, we should express kindness, patience and gentleness. Such a response gives the Holy Spirit time and space to bring about change in the one who has been taken captive.

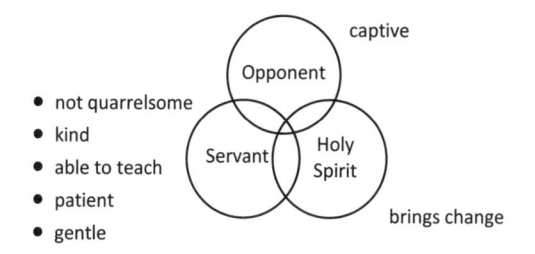

- not quarrelsome
- kind
- able to teach
- patient
- gentle

(Diagram: three intersecting circles labeled "Opponent", "Servant", and "Holy Spirit"; "captive" points to the Opponent circle and "brings change" points to the Holy Spirit circle.)

In the diagram above, there is a small area where all three circles intersect. Because of our mistaken belief

Suggestions for Spirit controlled living: 3 circles

that we can control another however, we our prone to overreach in order to bring about change. One of the most obvious ways we do this is by growing angry at the other person. You can see that such a posture has us overwhelming our opponent and impinging upon the Holy Spirit's territory.

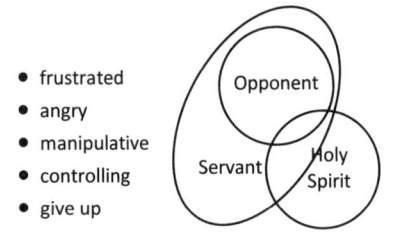

- frustrated
- angry
- manipulative
- controlling
- give up

When we do this, we are no longer treating the other person with kindness, gentleness or patience. Frustration, anger and manipulation have replaced those Christ-like qualities in our attempt to get the other person to do what we believe is best.

Christians can also be guilty of attempting to play the Holy Spirit's role in another's life. When this happens we move away from giving compassionate biblical counsel and replace that with our own opinion. Our counsel becomes guilt-driven and we use words to shame the other person.

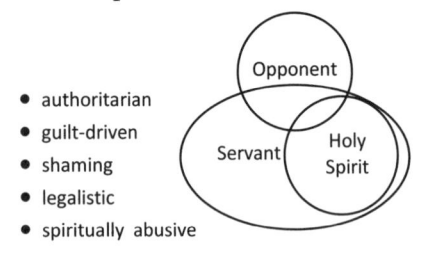

- authoritarian
- guilt-driven
- shaming
- legalistic
- spiritually abusive

The solution to both of these "overreaches" is to return to the list in 2 Timothy:

> And the Lord's servant must not be quarrelsome but kind to everyone, able to teach, patiently enduring evil, correcting his opponents with gentleness.

When we concentrate on the 2 Timothy list, we are acknowledging that we can't bring about genuine change in the heart of the captive. No amount of anger, guilt, or shame can bring about real change in another's heart. Only the Holy Spirit can set them free. However, we can be instruments in the Spirit's hand while he brings about change in the other person. Take a more careful look at those qualities from 2 Timothy 2:24-26.

- not quarrelsome
- kind to all
- able to teach
- patiently enduring evil
- gentleness

On a scale of 1-10, how would you grade yourself? What steps can you take today to grow in these Christ-like qualities as you overcome anger?

NOTES

1. http://en.wikipedia.org/wiki/Hayman_Fire

2. W.E. Vine, *Vine's Expository Dictionary of New Testament Words* (Mclean, VA: Macdonald Publishing, 1989).

3. Jeremiah 15:18

4. William Barclay, *The Letters to the Galatians and Ephesians. The Daily Study Bible Series* (Philadelphia, PA: The Westminster John Knox Press, 1976), 159.

5. http://www.goodreads.com/quotes/144557-resentment-is-like-drinking-poison-and-then-hoping-it-will

6. Romans 8:6

7. Ruth 1:1-5

8. Daniel 4:35

9. Luke 17:3-4

10. Psalm 100:5

11. Psalm 13, 73, 88, 142

12. Psalm 13:5-6; 73:23-28; 142:5. Even when Psalm 88 expresses complaint without remembering the attributes of God, it is bracketed by Psalm 87 and 89 which do (Psalm 87:2, 6; 89:1-2, 5-7, 9, 13-14, 21, 24, 26, 33, 35, 43).

13. The book of Philemon best expresses this posture. Fee and Stuart unpack this truth: "[Philemon] was an extremely delicate letter to write. Paul is explicitly asking forgiveness for a crime that deserved punishment (Onesimus's crime)—and implicitly for another crime that could have been brought before the proper authorities (Paul's harboring a runaway slave)...Did the letter work? ... Whether this Onesimus is the one who eventually became overseer of the church in Ephesus cannot be known for certain, but Christian tradition believed it so. We know about him from Ignatius, who, on his way to Rome to be martyred, wrote to the church in Ephesus: 'In God's name, therefore, I received your large congregation in the person of Onesimus, your bishop in this world, a man whose love is beyond words. My prayer is that you should love him in the Spirit of Jesus Christ and all be like him. Blessed is he who let you have such a bishop. You deserved it.' The gospel does things like that!" (Gordon Fee and Douglas Stuart, *How to Read the Bible Book by Book* (Grand Rapids, MI: Zondervan, 2002), 387).

14. Ephesians 4:32

15. G. Kittel, G. Friedrich, & G.W. Bromiley, *Theological Dictionary of the New Testament* (Grand Rapids, MI: W.B. Eerdmans, 1985).

16. This discovery was possible with the use of the Bible Word Study feature in Logos software.

17. Romans 2:8; Colossians 3:6; Revelation 14:10, 19; 15:1, 7; 16:1, 19; 19:15

18. Matthew 5:48; 2 Samuel 22:31

19. Luke 4:28; Acts 19:28; 2 Corinthians 12:20; Galatians 5:20; Ephesians 4:31; Colossians 3:8; Hebrews 11:27; Revelation 14:8; 18:3

20. Ephesians 4:31

21. Colossians 3:8

22. Galatians 5:19-20, NKJV

23. Romans 12:14-19, NKJV

24. *The Theological Dictionary of the*

New Testament states: "This term [*orge*] contains an element of awareness and even deliberation absent from *thymos*; [*orge* and words for which it serves as the root]... denotes an angry outburst which threatens to become lasting bitterness" (G. Kittel, G. Friedrich, & G.W. Bromiley, *Theological Dictionary of the New Testament* (Grand Rapids, MI: W.B. Eerdmans, 1985)).

25. William Barclay, *The Gospel of Matthew. The Daily Study Bible Series* (Philadelphia, PA: The Westminster John Knox Press, 1976), 138.

26. Jonah 4:5
27. Jonah 4:9
28. Jonah 4:9
29. Colossians 3:8
30. James 1:19-20

31. Consider these titles that Billboard.com listed as the top 50 love songs of all time: "You've lost that lovin' feelin'" by the Righteous Brothers (1965), "Can't help falling in love" by UB40 (1993), and "We found love" by Rihanna (2011). These titles, and others like them, reveal our popular culture's desire to see love as something that happens to you in contrast to a choice that you make (1 John 3:16).

32. Jonah 3:2
33. 2 Timothy 1:7
34. John 3:16
35. Matthew 26:31
36. Mark 14:45
37. John 18:14
38. John 19:6
39. John 17:23, 24
40. John 1:3
41. Colossians 1:17
42. Philippians 2:5-8
43. See pages 35-46 for the distinction between righteous and unrighteous anger.

44. G. Kittel, G.W. Bromiley, & G. Friedrich, Theological Dictionary of the New Testament (Grand Rapids, MI: Eerdmans, 1964), Vol. 3, 898.

45. W.E. Vine, *Vine's Expository Dictionary of New Testament Words* (Mclean, VA: MacDonald Publishing, 1989), Vol. 2, 103.

46. Exodus 12:30
47. Acts 23:9
48. James 1:19-20
49. Romans 12:16

50. Steven Covey, *The Seven Habits of Highly Effective People* (New York, NY: Free Press, 1989).

51. Romans 12:16
52. Proverbs 10:19
53. Proverbs 17:27
54. Proverbs 18:13
55. http://definitions.uslegal.com/s/slander/

56. Ephesians 4:25 points out that there are two ways to be dishonest: "Therefore, having (1) put away falsehood, let each one of you (2) speak the truth to his neighbor." The first occurrence refers to telling an untruth when asked. But the second occurrence appears to be more proactive. It warns us not to withhold truth if the listener would have a need to know. On that occurrence, we don't wait to be asked—we speak truth.

57. Luke 17:4
58. 1 Peter 4:8
59. John 1:17
60. Ephesians 4:29
61. 1 Corinthians 13:7
62. Ephesians 4:29
63. http://definitions.uslegal.com/m/malice/

64. For instance, intent is one of the elements that must be demonstrated to move a manslaughter charge to a murder charge.

65. Romans 1:29; 1 Corinthians 5:8

66. Romans 12:19-21

67. Genesis 18:25

68. Romans 6:16

69. W.E. Vine, *Vine's Expository Dictionary of New Testament Words* (Mclean, VA: Macdonald Publishing, 1989).

70. Galatians 5:1

71. Philippians 4:13

72. Romans 6:16

73. Galatians 5:13

74. Ezekiel 36:26

75. 2 Corinthians 10:5; Matthew 6:33

76. Psalm 37:4; Philippians 4:4

77. Romans 6:16; 12:2

78. This is my imaginative retelling of the Jesus' purging of the temple. The historical record is found in Mark 11:15-19.

79. Mark 11:11

80. Mark 11:15

81. Mark 11:17

82. John 2:17; Mark 3:5

83. 1 John 3:5

84. http://www.julianspriggs.com/pages/annascaiaphas.aspx

85. Mark 10:45

86. Psalm 68:5-6

87. Mark 10:44-45

88. Mathew 21:12; Mark 11:15

89. Conversation about righteous anger with Joe Schenke.

90. Mark 11:11

91. Mark 11:12, 15

92. Ephesians 4:31

93. David Powlison, *Anger: Escaping the Maze* (Phillipsburg, NJ: R&R Publishing, 2000).

94. Matthew 21:13

95. Isaiah 56:6

96. ibid.

97. Robert Jones, *Uprooting Anger: biblical help for a common problem* (Phillipsburg, NJ: R&R Publishing, 2005).

98. Luke 9:58

99. Luke 9:44

100. Luke 9:46-48

101. James 4:1-4

102. Philippians 2:5-8

103. 1 Peter 2:23

104. ibid.

105. Luke 9:22

106. Luke 9:24-25

107. Hebrews 12:2

108. Romans 5:3-5

109. Romans 8:28-29

110. Mark 14:56

111. Luke 11:14-18

112. Matthew 4:1-14

113. Mark 5:9

114. Mark 5:10

115. Luke 11:17-19

116. Luke 11:1-2, 9-10

117. Galatians 5:16, 18, 25

118. Galatians 5:19-21

119. Galatians 5:22-23

120. Philippians 4:9

121. 2 Corinthians 10:5

122. Ephesians 4:26-27

123. Ephesians 6:12

124. 2 Corinthians 10:3-4

125. Ephesians 6:11, 13, 14

126. James 1:20

127. Proverbs 14:17, 29; 16:32

128. Ephesians 6:14-17

129. John 8:44

130. Wayne Grudem, *Systematic Theology: an Introduction to Biblical Doctrine* (Grand Rapids, MI: Inter-

varsity Press; Zondervan Publishing House, 2004), 442.

131. Milton Vincent, *The Gospel Primer* (Bemidji, MN: Focus Publishing, 2008).

132. John MacArthur, *The MacArthur Study Bible* (Wheaton, IL: Crossway Books, 1997).

133. Max Anders, *The Holman New Testament Commentary: Galatians-Colossians* (Nashville, TN: Broadman & Holman Publishers, 1999), 190.

134. James 4:1-4

135. Don Whitney, *Spiritual Disciplines* (Colorado Springs, CO: Navpress, 1991), 44.

136. E.D. Radmacher, R.B. Allen, & H.W. House, *The Nelson Study Bible* (Nashville, TN: Nelsons Publishers, 1997).

137. Habakkuk 3:17-19

138. https://www.navigators.org/www_navigators_org/media/navigators/tools/Resources/Praying-the-Names-of-God-The-Navigators.pdf

139. James 1:19-20

About the Author

Phil Moser is the author of the Biblical Strategies series. He is a pastor, frequent blogger (philmoser.com) and conference speaker. He holds a degree in Business Management, and earned his Masters of Divinity from The Master's Seminary, Sun Valley, California. He presently serves as the teaching pastor of Fellowship Bible Church in Mullica Hill, New Jersey. He has served as an adjunct professor teaching the Bible, theology, apologetics, homiletics, and counseling in Albania, Korea, Germany, Hungary and Ukraine.

Resources from Biblical Strategies

Just Like Jesus: biblical strategies for growing well

Fighting the Fire: biblical strategies for overcoming anger

Dead End Desire: biblical strategies for overcoming self-pity

Taking Back Time: biblical strategies for overcoming procrastination

Safe in the Storm: biblical strategies for overcoming anxiety

Discerning the Deception: biblical strategies for overcoming sexual temptation

Biblical Strategies
How you get to where God's taking you.
BiblicalStrategies.com